HAIR
LIKE
A FOX

DANNY RODDY

DISCLAIMER

The information provided in this book should not be construed as personal medical advice or instruction. No action should be taken based solely on the contents of this book. Readers should consult appropriate health "authorities" on any matter relating to their health and well-being. The information and opinions provided here are believed to be accurate and sound, based on the best judgment available to the author, but readers who fail to consult appropriate health "authorities" assume the risk of any injuries. Use of the suggestions and other information contained in this book is at the sole choice and risk of the reader.
Your health is in your own hands.

ACKNOWLEDGMENTS

First and foremost, I would like to thank Andrew Kim and Evan Winchester for the monumental task of editing this book. Among my friends whose help has made a real difference, I would like to mention: Rob Turner, Phil, Cliff McCrary and Nick Warcholak. From a foundational perspective, I warmly acknowledge the profound influence of Raymond Peat, PhD.

CONTENTS

Acknowledgments   i

1   Introduction   1

2   Who am I? Why am I Here?   Pg 3

3   The Androgen Hypothesis   Pg 16

4   A Shift in Paradigm   Pg 25

5   A Bioenergetic View of Pattern Hair Loss   Pg 34

6   A Bioenergetic View of Estrogen   Pg 44

7   A Bioenergetic View of Serotonin   Pg 58

8   A Bioenergetic View of The "Essential Fatty   Pg 67
    Acids"

9   Steps Toward a Logical "Pro-Hair" Lifestyle   Pg 79

10 The Future   Pg 99

INTRODUCTION, OR: WHY YOUR DOCTOR DOESN'T CARE ABOUT YOU

"Without self knowledge, without understanding the working and functions of his machine, man cannot be free, he cannot govern himself and he will always remain a slave."

—G. I. Gurdjieff

Listen, your doctor doesn't care about you.

And you know what your doctor really doesn't care about? Your hair.

If you're feeling blue about the clog you found in your shower drain this morning, your doctor will be happy to write you a prescription for an antidepressant, but don't expect it to do anything for your impending baldness. For that, you'll need an FDA-approved drug with the potential side effect of permanent chemical castration. Ladies, you will have the additional option of taking birth control, increasing the likelihood of miscarriage, stroke, osteoporosis and tissue degeneration (i.e., rapid aging).

My physician friends will no doubt take issue with the above, and although I'm being slightly hyperbolic, I'm being mostly sincere. Reversing pattern baldness requires a radically different context for viewing health problems than most physicians are capable of accepting.

Acknowledging the information in this book as accurate would mean that doctors are contributing to illness by performing X-rays, increasing the risk of cancer, stroke, osteoporosis, and heart attack in women by prescribing birth control, or committing acts of criminal negligence by handing out serotonin reuptake inhibitors (SSRIs) like Tic Tacs.

The booming market of "alternative physicians" is not much better. While they are usually hip to the problems with birth control (thanks Suzanne Somers), they subscribe to the same fundamental errors in medicine that make MDs so dangerous. Instead of using birth control, they use phytoestrogens and estrogen-replacement therapy. Instead of prescribing SSRIs, they use supplements containing 5-HTP and tryptophan. Same shit, more price gouging.

Over the last decade, I have searched for a simple physiological solution for reversing "male-pattern baldness." I have reviewed the work of Peat, Selye, Szent-Györgyi, Warburg, Barnes, Williams, and many others who have revolutionized biology and helped shape a realistic view of the organism. Their work allowed me to shed several preconceived ideas about baldness (i.e., that it is caused by "bad genes" and "male" hormones) and set a new context for why pattern baldness occurs and simple, yet effective methods for reversing it.

It's time to take your health into your own hands and become your own expert. Think for yourself and question authority. Do whatever it takes to find the best information available. No one will figure this out for you, but this book will give you a head start.

WHO AM I? WHY AM I HERE?

"I start with trying to make a context clear, because everyone's context is different, and meanings change when they are learned. Ideally, things should make no sense until they make the right sense."
—Raymond Peat, PhD

This is where I begin my story; a story that I never thought I would be sharing with the public, and definitely not in a book I would be writing about pattern baldness.

I had a much different life planned out for myself. While most of my friends were academics, I was never a good student because I could never wrap my head around the concept of "homework." However, while I wasn't serious about my education, I was as serious as a heart attack about my musical endeavors.

I learned to play the bass guitar in my early teens, which led to playing in a series of rock bands with friends. Naturally, because I wasn't that great at anything else, I thought I would become a successful musician. Much to my amazement that actually happened, and I eventually found myself touring around the world with four of my best friends on Island Def Jam's tab. But I'm getting ahead of myself. Before we navigate through the course of events that led me to writing this book, I should probably start from the very beginning.

The Wonder Years

As a young child, I remember fearing baldness. I know, that sounds nutty but it's true. And I can remember two instances that made me feel that way.

The first event happened when I was a teenager on a weeknight while hunting my cat, Sniffles, with a Nerf gun. My dad came home that evening and I vividly remember him explaining to my Mom his distaste for a "bald idiot" that he worked with. It was rare for my Dad to talk ill of anyone, so I'm guessing that this made quite an impression on me, as I aligned my sights on Sniffles in the hallway.

The second event, around the same time, happened when my sisters and I found a picture of my deceased Grandpa, which revealed that he was completely bald. My sisters both commented on how that meant that I had "the bald gene" and that I, too, would lose my hair.

These two events instilled hair-fear in me at an age when all I wanted to do was watch Batman and listen to Prince. Would I become the "bald idiot" that my father spoke of? Would anyone ever love me if I lost my beautiful brown locks? These questions festered in the back of my mind. But luckily, I was able to suppress them to the darkest nether regions of my psyche; that is, until high school.

Besides rejecting the idea of homework, I attribute my dismal high school performance to testing anxiety. No matter how well I thought I knew the material, I would crumble into a fine micronized powder on test day under the pressure.

This was especially apparent during final exams during my senior year of high school. While taking a test on a book I hadn't even read, I remember rubbing my scalp to try to stimulate some brain activity. While the method had no effect on my test score, it did produce a near endless amount of dandruff and falling hair. The adolescent feelings about baldness that I had buried in the deepest recesses of my mind had abruptly reemerged, like a bat out of hell. After high school, at the young age of 19, I was already thinking about ways in which I could stop my inevitable hair loss.

Don't Mind My Watery Semen

Initially, I tried generic supplements from my local grocery store. Though I felt proactive, I really wasn't sure if the supplements were doing anything, as any kind of stress would continue to cause my dandruff and hair loss to get worse.

While my struggle with how to go about treating my hair loss became more complex, my career as a musician was burgeoning. During my first year of community college, my buddy contacted me to ask if I wanted to leave my current band to join another band that not only was already signed to an independent label, but also had a van that was ready for touring and a lead vocalist that I thought was amazing. I can't do justice to how excited I felt about this opportunity so suffice it to say here, I dropped to my knees overwhelmed with joy.

This, of course, caused me to become even more serious about my hair loss, which is actually a theme to the narrative of my life. I soon ditched whatever supplement I was taking at the time and went straight for the big gun: Propecia.

I made an appointment for the nearest endocrinologist who performed blood work for testosterone and dihydrotestosterone (DHT), whereupon obtaining the results, officially diagnosed me with what I already knew: I was losing hair from the front and top of my scalp in the typical "male pattern baldness" fashion. He wrote me a prescription for Propecia, and I immediately drove to the pharmacy to fill it. When I returned home from the doctor's office I felt a temporary sense of serenity. I had done it; I had secured my right as an American to keep my hair through the use of a high-powered pharmaceutical drug.

However, after a few months of taking Propecia, something happened. The spontaneous erections I had everyday since I was a young rapscallion disappeared. To add to the paranormal activity, ejaculating during intercourse became near impossible, causing me to have to explain to attractive women why I was going limp inside them. When I was able to ejaculate, my semen quality was visibly different, taking on a water-like consistency.

If someone had told me that impotence was the price I had to pay to keep my hair for the rest of my life, I probably would have accepted those terms; but this was unfortunately not the case. My hair was not doing well. I was still a victim to stressful situations that worsened my hair loss and dandruff. And to make matters even worse, my scalp began to physically hurt.

I'm not sure if it was the drug, my lack of ability to have relations with women, or the fact that my hair loss seemed to go into overdrive, but all of the events that had transpired up until this point had culminated into an overwhelming sense of doom. I began experiencing mini-panic attacks, fearing for my future aesthetically as a musician.

Upon eventually regaining my composure, I once again became proactive and turned to the Internet to see whether other people were experiencing the side effects I was on Propecia. Thirty minutes of perusing propeciasideeffects.com revealed that not only were all the side effects I was experiencing common, but also that some men experienced those side effects for life – even after stopping Propecia. My heart sank. I took my stash of Propecia and dropped it in the trash. I prayed that the drug's effects were reversible. Lucky for me, after a few months my libido and semen quality returned to normal.

Feeling horrible and not knowing what I was going to do next, it was back to the drawing board.

The "Natural" Route

My Propecia experience shook me to my core. Like many others in my situation who have had poor experiences with pharmaceutical drugs, I was sure that there had to be more effective natural alternatives for my problem. My suspicions were confirmed when I uncovered the community over at regrowth.com. Like any online forum, there were a few members that had very strong opinions about how to go about treating pattern hair loss "naturally." The member with the strongest opinions, or rather the most well thought out opinions, was a gentleman named Brian Simonis who went by the handle, "Immortalhair."

Brian was very active on the forum, but also ran a non-profit website that kept everyone up to date on his hair loss research. His main message was that pattern hair loss was more complex than the pharmaceutical companies were suggesting, and that hair loss was a systemic problem – not merely a compartmentalized one.

Brian's information and knowledge on the topic blew my mind. While I didn't understand everything Brian was saying, I became obsessed with his regimen, taking notes along the way and soaking up as much information as I could.

While his regimen originally contained a few "core" supplements and a dozen or so "ancillary" supplements, I adopted the entire regimen literally overnight. I methodically filled pill baggies with exactly enough supplements to get me through the day, and became somewhat fanatical about it. Often, I would refuse to eat if I had forgotten my supplements.

Looking back, I can't say why my fanaticism over this

regimen lasted for as long as it did because at no point did I have noticeable improvements in the hair department. As with Propecia, I still had dandruff and I still experienced hair loss when I was under stress.

After a year of heavy-duty supplementation, I had an epiphany. If the supplements I was taking were supporting an internal environment for hair growth, couldn't a good diet accomplish the same thing? The answer, as I methodically discovered, was invariably yes. But what was the diet that best supported hair growth?

The Hair Destroying Diet

After a few weeks of exploring what the best diet would be, I decided to adopt what I believed to be the healthiest of diets; and that diet was veganism. My days consisted of green smoothies, rice noodles, garbanzo beans, tempeh, and seitan. I limited fruit and processed sugar and consumed a wide array of exotic vegetables (e.g., kale, bok choy, mustard greens). Adhering to this restrictive diet was easy for me to do as long as I thought it was going to regrow my hair.

Several months passed and my lean 150 lb. body wasted away to an emaciated 110 lbs. I was sick, on edge, couldn't sleep, and my libido was nonexistent.

Although my friends and family were terribly worried, none of them could understand (or know) why I was doing what I was doing. How would I explain to them how much my hair meant to me? Even more troubling, how would I express my conviction that only the "perfect diet" would resolve my untimely hair loss?

Luckily, I decided to employ these wacky dietary changes when stress from the band was at its peak. Takota, my band, was being courted by every major label in the music industry and we were playing showcases every weekend for record executives interested in signing the band. At one point we even played for Jay-Z.

After our second self-funded tour to Europe, we decided to sign with Island Def Jam and the first step was to record a new record. While most bands would stop playing shows to focus on recording, our management actively started booking shows throughout the west coast. This unrelenting regimen of recording and touring took its toll on the entire band and practically killed me. Living on McDonald's side salads and apples, I was more malnourished then I had ever been. Upon arriving in San Francisco for an important show, my fragility became apparent to everyone, including myself.

During the "load-in," the rhythm guitar player and I split the responsibility of carrying my bass speaker – one of the heaviest pieces of gear we owned. Normally, the bass cabinet was easy to move with a bandmates help. However, I struggled, as my withered 110 lb. frame wasn't exactly operating like a high-performance machine. As we lugged the speaker down a flight of stairs, I fell backwards, dropping the cabinet in front of everyone.

I was weak, emotionally and physically. When we arrived home from the tour, much to the surprise of everyone, I gave up veganism and went back to the drawing board, again.

The 110 lb. Bodybuilder

As I searched for a new solution to my problem, I stumbled upon an online forum filled with physiology-obsessed bodybuilders. Instead of relying on the media's idea of what it meant to be healthy, the majority of the content on the site encouraged self-experimentation and lab testing.

While the conversation ranged from hormones and diet, to self-reported cases of getting jacked using experimental pharmaceutical approaches, the back and forth was mostly about the serious problems these guys were having—the kinds of problems that make your most hardcore Paleo friend look like a low-post noob. One forum member got in a fight with his girlfriend, punched her in the face, and then came online to tell everyone he was about to pull a Weekend at Bernie's on us.

Besides the occasional attempted-suicide, being a part of the forum was rewarding, especially when members would post their lab work for the entire forum to evaluate. And because these guys were seasoned veterans at this, their labs included multiple blood and urine panels for the same markers to avoid lab inaccuracies. Over time, an obvious trend emerged: despite these Adonis-physiqued bodybuilders' most heroic efforts to "support their adrenals," become "essential fatty acid" replete, and overcome various stressors with herbal "anti-stress" adaptogens, nothing got these guys to where they wanted to be.

At a certain point, it became obvious that the hormones these gentlemen found to be anomalous in lab work (e.g., estrogen, prolactin, etc.) were the same hormones Brian Simonis had mentioned were involved in the pathology of pattern baldness. This realization motivated me to employ extensive changes to my regimen.

I employed lab testing on myself, utilized hormonal replacement therapy, experimented with more exotic supplements, and even flew out to Michigan to see a specialist. My regimen went from simple to extremely complex, requiring me to carry multiple baggies full of pills, gels, and creams on tour, for example. I learned an incredible amount about myself in a short period of time, but like the other gentlemen on the forum, after a lengthy period of time, and an extreme amount of effort, I wasn't where I wanted to be.

I gave up most of my supplements and medications and redirected my attention on a compelling argument that kept creeping up on the forum; the idea that insulin resistance caused most hormone imbalances, and that excessive carbohydrate consumption caused insulin resistance.

I began exploring the depths of the low-carb world, and eventually came to believe that the overconsumption of carbohydrates was central in most all disease states, including baldness, which was associated with insulin resistance.

I decided to experiment with carbohydrate restriction, which worked well. I felt calmer, slept better, and felt less hunger. I interpreted all these signs as positive, and further tinkered with the amounts of fat and carbohydrate in my diet in order to find my optimal ratio.

Soon after, I was introduced to the concept of "evolutionary" (e.g., Paleo, caveman, primal) nutrition. This concept, which as far as I can tell started with the publication of Ray Audette's *Neanderthin*, was based on the idea of mimicking the internal metabolic conditions under which our ancestors had supposedly evolved.

This "evolutionary" approach to eating dovetailed nicely with the current success I was having with carbohydrate restriction. The difference was the exclusion of "Neolithic" foods, such as dairy and grains, in favor of meat, vegetables, and, in some cases, fruit and starchy tubers.

Although I found the evolutionary approach to eating to be extremely compelling, I knew that low-carbohydrate diets didn't reverse pattern baldness in most cases. However, because of my context – that carbohydrates raise insulin, and that the exposure to insulin causes nearly all the diseases of civilization – I came to the conclusion that people with pattern hair loss had to be consuming excessive amounts of carbohydrates, disregarding what I knew from my own experience and observations.

Later on, confirmation bias reared its ugly head as I acquiescently read a snippet from a book by the famous Arctic explorer Vilhjalmur Stefansson called *Not By Bread Alone*, in which he described the hair-supporting effects of an all-meat diet. Stefansson had convinced The American

Meat Institute to fund a yearlong all-meat diet study supervised by a panel of prestigious doctors. When Stefansson and his partner, Karsten Andersen, embarked on the diet, they were closely monitored while they stayed at Bellevue hospital in New York.

Their diets contained modest amounts of fat with smaller portions of lean meat in quantities sufficient to bring about satiety. Stefansson averaged about 2,650 calories a day, consisting of 2,100 calories of fat and 550 of protein; Andersen averaged about 2,620 calories a day, consisting of 2,110 calories of fat and 510 of protein.

At the end of the Bellevue study the only surprising element was how anticlimactic the results were. Stefansson had lost ten pounds, despite the fact that he was lean to begin with. Neither Karsten nor Stefansson developed scurvy, and Karsten reported that his digestive problems had disappeared, his immune system had improved, and that his hair had stopped falling out.

This was all I needed to hear. I began consuming an all meat and water diet the next day, in what became an experiment that lasted for nearly two years.

The All-Meat Years

You would think that consuming a diet of meat and water would be all bad, and mostly it was, but I immediately noticed several health improvements. Initially, I noticed that my hair benefitted. Inflammation of scalp decreased, dandruff disappeared, and my hair just felt resilient.

The weird part was that I actually liked eating just one thing. I enjoyed telling people that I ate only meat and water, and enjoyed explaining it even more. Meat was easy to get on tour and, believe it or not, I never got sick of eating ribeyes.

To keep my mind off the stress of record politics, which had become completely draining at that point, I intermittently weblogged about my experience. Along with Charles Washington, who should probably take credit for advancing the zero-carb movement, I experienced a considerable amount of online traffic from those interested in my experiences eating only meat.

While the first year went pretty well, the second year began my rapid decent into degeneration. I began experiencing some new (and old) symptoms – a dramatic lack of libido, extreme fatigue, cold intolerance, un-restful sleep and, in general, a sour disposition.

The second year is also when I became somewhat serious with a former girlfriend. My self-experimentation not only affected me, but her as well. For instance, she planned a trip to a museum on a Sunday I had off from work and band practice. I remember being so physically exhausted (from being alive) that I could barely walk up the steps to enter the museum. She later told me that she wanted to have sport sex in an abandoned area in the museum, but knew that I wouldn't have been able to because of how frail I had become.

Besides missing out on sport sex, I probably developed scurvy, too. I remember waking up one morning and finding my legs covered in petechiae, which are small red pustules. While aesthetically disgusting, the real bummer was that it affected my ability to walk. I worked at a retail store at the time, and I remember my boss being disturbed at how physically ill I had become.

For one reason or another I simply dealt with these symptoms for a matter of weeks before I came to the realization that I was extremely malnourished. Luckily, eating more food seemed to make the problems go away.

You would have thought that a mild case of the ol' scurvy would have ended my all-meat adventure, but you would be wrong. The clincher was actually the implosion of my relationship that forced me to view my dietary habits from another angle.

To add to the stress of breaking up with my girlfriend,

it was about this time that the long-time guitarist of the band decided to bail. This was a thermonuclear event, and caused me to question my desire to play music as well as my capacity to be a musician. Immediately after my bandmate's departure, our distraught singer asked everyone in the room to assure him that they were never going to leave. He looked at me and I instantly broke down. I told him that I couldn't reassure him and that I had mentally "checked out" a while ago. My passion for nutrition and genuine disinterest in the music industry had come to a tipping point. I cared more about solving the riddle of pattern baldness than the years of my life I devoted to promoting, playing shows, writing music, recording, and touring.

At this point, I was girlfriend-less, band-less, and my bulletproof idea of eating meat and water for two years left me in pretty terrible shape. Even worse was that I had nothing in the pipeline. I wasn't sure of what to do next.

After a few months of moping around and a dash of self-loathing, I picked myself up off the floor and began studying the work of Raymond Peat, PhD. Peat was considered to be quite the quack in the "evolutionary" circle I ran with, which only served to increase my curiosity and desire to read his work that much more.

When Danny Met Ray

Over the course of three years, I found Dr. Peat's comprehensive view of the organism to be nothing short of visionary. For example, someone could spend the rest of their life reading PubMed and not paint a meaningful picture of how the body works. The bioenergetic context Dr. Peat has been elucidating over the last four decades, connecting the work of Otto Warburg, Albert Szent-Györgyi, Gilbert Ling and others in an elegant easy-to-understand way is simply awe-inspiring.

Dr. Peat's work helped me set a new context for

engaging in self-experimentation and allowed me to reach a point where I was satisfied with my health. For the first time in what felt like a decade, my hands and feet became warm, my libido increased to that of my teens, and my hair loss completely arrested.

Dr. Peat's work surrounds his thesis, which states that energy and structure are interdependent at every level. While I deemed statements like these to be esoteric in the beginning, as my knowledge and understanding of Dr. Peat's work evolved, they later became empowering, and an indispensable template for understanding health, disease, nutrition and hair loss.

The Moral: Trust No One, Including Me

If my near-decade long journey taught me anything, it was to question everything and trust no one. In fact, this is the same phrase that currently sits at the footer of my website and has sat there since its conception.

While I was incredibly naïve when I began my journey, I quickly came to the realization that no one was going to fix my health for me. What allowed me to overcome my health problems were self-experimentation and seeking out what I deemed to be the best information available.

This sentiment is at odds with many of my peers, however, as most of them would prefer to adhere to their doctors' orders and not involve themselves in technical matters. Normally, I wouldn't have a problem with this, but unfortunately, in the case of pattern baldness, following advice from your doctor may result in permanent erectile dysfunction, gynecomastia (male breast growth), or suicide. And while these side effects are horrific, they are just part of the system that sustains itself through incompetence, negligence, and the real world fiction that the food and drug administration (FDA) has the public's best interest at heart.

THE ANDROGEN HYPOTHESIS

"Castration at early ages affords a reliable form of therapy, but one in which the cure is worse than the disease."
—Dr. James B. Hamilton

In 1942 Dr. James B. Hamilton changed the course of hair loss research with his groundbreaking study in a group of 104 men who failed to mature sexually (i.e., eunuchs or eunachoids).[1] Both young and old, the men were unified by testicular insufficiency, which Dr. Hamilton found to give rise to three anomalies:

1) A lack of balding and retention of all scalp hair.
2) Less sebaceous gland activity, compared to normal men of comparable age, that resulted in a reduced oiliness of the face, hair, and scalp and a complete lack of acne.
3) Dandruff that was either absent or present in such small amounts such that only a few white flakes could be brushed off from the scalp. In stark contrast, mature young men of the same age had copious amounts of dandruff.

Faced with the obvious correlation between castration

and hair retention, Dr. Hamilton administered "male" hormone injections (i.e., testosterone propionate) to men who were not bald. Upon receiving these injections, those with a family history of baldness experienced a pronounced loss of hair; however, halting the treatment ceased all further hair loss. In castrates who received the same injections without interruption, not only was hair loss induced, but it also continued unabated.

A discrepancy that arose from these experiments as to the role of testosterone in hair loss was that the amount of testosterone that was required to induce baldness in the castrates did not exceed the amounts secreted by the testes of the average young, healthy male with hair.

No matter how strong the inherited physiological state, hair loss would not result if "inciting agents," which Hamilton believed to be "male" androgens, were missing. This was evidenced by old eunuchs who were castrated prior to sexual maturation that retained their prepubertal hairlines and "luxuriant scalp hair".

Thirty-two years after Dr. Hamilton's experiments with the eunuchs came a discovery that not only led to a set of cultural stereotypes about baldness, but also to a drug that for some men would alter the course of their lives forever.

The DHT Connection

In 1974, Dr. Julianne Imperato-McGinley, an endocrinologist at Cornell, travelled to the Dominican Republic to observe a remote mountain village with a population of male pseudohermaphrodites called the Guevedoces ("penis at 12 years").[2] Appearing sexually ambiguous at birth, the Guevedoces were raised as girls. But during puberty, they developed external genitalia, increased muscle mass, and deep voices. Similar to Dr. Hamilton's eunuchs, the Guevedoces were conspicuously free of pattern baldness and acne.

The affected males were found to have normal plasma

testosterone concentrations, but were deficient in dihydrotestosterone (DHT), a derivative of testosterone. Upon further research, Dr. Imperato-McGinely's group ended up discovering the first inherited disorder of steroid hormone metabolism, a deficiency of the 5-alpha reductase enzyme (5-AR) that converts testosterone into DHT. Because the Guevedoces had normal levels of testosterone in their blood, Dr. Imperato-McGinely's group surmised that DHT, rather than testosterone, had to be responsible for bringing about baldness.

Regardless of the implications of Imperato-McGinley's research, it wouldn't have mattered much in the grand scheme of things. Normally, gathering data and forming intelligent hypotheses would lead to various tests, which would eventually eliminate mistaken ones. However, in the case of pattern baldness, the virtue of science was shortchanged when the pharmaceutical companies stepped in.

Becoming The Castrate

In 1974, a monograph of a conference Dr. Imperato McGinley spoke at landed on the desk of Merck pharmaceutical's research chief, Dr. Vagelos. Vagelos was intrigued by Imperato-McGinley's research and more specifically by her notation that the prostate glands of those with inherited 5-AR deficiency remained small throughout life. Dr. Vagelos thought that if Merck could mimic the Guevedoces' 5-AR deficiency with a drug, it might have a product for the market of 15 million American men suffering from enlarged prostate glands (benign prostate hyperplasia or BPH), an embarrassing and often painful condition that can block urine flow, interrupt sleep and predispose to serious infections.

Merck spearheaded the concept, eventually producing Finasteride (marketed as Proscar), a type-II 5-alpha-reductase inhibitor that reduces, quite significantly, the concentrations of DHT in the body. Finasteride, as a side effect, also regrew hair. Merck lowered the dose of Proscar from 5mg to 1mg, and, in 1997, introduced the world to Propecia – the first FDA-approved drug for male-pattern baldness – to immediate popularity. Despite this, Finasteride has been continuously steeped in controversy due to its unconscionable side effects.

Some of the most serious side effects that have been attributed to the use of Finasteride include, but are not limited to, the following:

- Gynecomastia[3]
- Depression[4]
- Suicide[5]

Finasteride is potent in that the typical 1 mg dose prescribed to patients by physicians for male pattern baldness can reduce DHT levels by about 70% within 24 hours.[6] DHT is anywhere from 4 to 10 times as potent as testosterone, and normally maintains male secondary sex characteristics, as well as the ability to become sexually aroused.

While all these symptoms are obviously disturbing, the side effect that most men find to be particularly egregious and horrifying is permanent erectile dysfunction. Visiting websites such as propeciasideeffects.com or propeciahelp.com will reveal many anecdotes of men who are now unable to recover their ability to obtain an erection after using the drug for only a short period of time. After years of allegations, Merck finally responded by updating the package insert that accompanies Finasteride, stating therein that Finasteride could cause "sexual dysfunction that continued after discontinuation of treatment, including erectile dysfunction, decreased libido and ejaculation disorders (e.g. reduced ejaculate volume)."[7]

Independent research on the side effects of Finasteride found that in a small study of 72 participants, 94%

developed low libido, 92% developed erectile dysfunction, 92% developed decreased arousal, and 69% developed problems with orgasm.[8]

These problems would maybe be tolerable, if only the use of Finasteride was guaranteed in all cases to restore hair growth; or at least to slow the progression of hair loss. But that's unfortunately not the case. When compared to Hamilton's eunuchs and Dr. Imperato-McGinley's pseudohermaphrodites, all of whom were protected from baldness 100 percent of the time, Finasteride is effective for only about 40 percent of those who take it, suggesting that there are other factors at play in pattern baldness.

The Androgen Paradox?

Nearly a decade after his original discovery, Hamilton cast doubt on his own findings, invoking the word "paradox" to explain the role of "male" hormones in baldness. Hamilton's paradox came in the form of an observation that baldness increased in severity and frequency with age, whereas the stimulating agents (i.e., "male" androgens) very often decreased with age.[9]

This paradox is further supported by the fact that the androgens are known to produce long, thick, pigmented scalp hairs in youth, yet produce baldness later in life. How could the androgens be responsible for vigorously growing hair during adolescence and later for terminating hair growth in adulthood when the concentrations of the androgens decrease?

To preface the answer to that question, it should be noted that the word "paradox" is usually employed when things become unimaginable in medical culture. For instance, when it is found that a population that consumes what is deemed to be in our society excessive amounts of cholesterol and saturated fat is virtually free of heart disease (e.g., Inuit); or when it is found that restricting dietary salt has a negligible (clinically insignificant) effect on a person's blood pressure; or when it is found that high intakes of calcium does not increase the risk for errant calcification processes (e.g., Masai), but rather protects against it. What seems paradoxical, in reality, reveals basic errors in the understanding of physiology propagated by medical dogmatists.

In the case of the "androgen paradox", the theory is reconciled with a bit of post hoc reasoning and physiological gymnastics: balding men aren't necessarily producing more androgens; they're simply more sensitive to them because of an inherited genetic defect.

When scrutiny is applied, this "sensitivity" argument becomes a stretch. Although there are no precise statistics, the incidence of pattern baldness in whites is often quoted as approaching 100 percent;[10] less grandiose estimates suggest that half of all men and women above 40 experience pattern hair loss.[11] Wouldn't these kinds of statistics require an impossibly high rate of gene mutation?

Moreover, balding is increasingly becoming a metabolic marker for future and current health problems, including metabolic syndrome,[12] insulin resistance,[13,14] hypertension,[15,16] polycystic ovarian syndrome,[17,18] heart disease,[19] and cancer.[20] How does an 'enhanced sensitivity to androgens in the scalp' help to explain the association between hair loss and these health problems?

Finally, while heavily relied upon to explain the genesis of balding in men, this theory is completely jettisoned in other cases of "male-pattern baldness". For instance "male-pattern" hair loss is observed in females (female androgenic alopecia),[21] in newborns during the first year of life,[22] women taking oral contraceptives,[23] postpartum mothers,[24] post-menopausal women,[25] and senescent alopecia (hair loss in those over 50 years of age).[26] These situations are believed to be age-related or androgen-independent or both. A "genetic sensitivity to androgens in the scalp" isn't usually invoked. Why is the aging male subjected to the androgen hypothesis, while children, women and the elderly are subject to a completely different theory? These errors in reasoning obviously represent a broader problem in our medical culture — a culture that discounts the entirety of an individual in favor of fragmentation and reductionism.

Androgens or Aging?

There is a strong commitment to the androgen hypothesis in the research on balding that never fails to mention the pioneering work of Dr. Hamilton. While I think Dr. Hamilton's work was incomplete, and essentially perverted to establish a doctrine of pattern hair loss, even he suspected that factors may supersede the role of androgens in baldness:

> The suspicion arises that androgens are not the 'directly causative' agent in baldness, but only one member—albeit a frequently effective one—of a family of remote causes that affect local areas capable of reacting in a special manner.[27]

Seven decades later, it's safe to say that androgens are not the "directly causative" agents in baldness. Rather, like other multicellular tissues, the function and longevity of the hair follicle is dependent on the energetic state of the cells that make up its structure. Pattern baldness in both sexes is characterized by a shift from "efficient" to "inefficient" cellular energy metabolism, evidenced by an increase in the adaptive "stress" substances. Over time, these adaptive "stress" substances cause pathological changes in the scalp, including the accumulation of mucopolysaccharides, deranged calcification processes, reduced follicular blood flow, hypoxia, oxidative stress, and mitochondrial dysfunction, all of which predispose to temporary or permanent baldness. These changes just so happen to be the same changes seen in the tissues of aging organisms; we now have a rational starting point for a new paradigm.

References

1. Hamilton, J.B. Male hormone stimulation is prerequisite and an incitant in common baldness. Am J Anat 71:451-480 1942
2. Imperato-McGinley, J. et al. Steroid 5alpha-reductase deficiency in man: an inherited form of male pseudohermaphroditism. Science. 1974 Dec 27;186(4170):1213-5.
3. Ramot, Y. et al. Finasteride induced Gynecomastia: Case report and Review of the Literature. Int J Trichology. 2009 Jan-Jun; 1(1): 27–29.
4. Rahimi-Ardabili, B. et al. Finasteride induced depression: a prospective study. BMC Clin Pharmacol. 2006 Oct 7;6:7.
5. Irwig, M.S. Depressive symptoms and suicidal thoughts among former users of finasteride with persistent sexual side effects. J Clin Psychiatry. 2012 Sep;73(9):1220-3.
6. Vermeulen, A., et al. Hormonal effects of a 5 alpha-reductase inhibitor (finasteride) on hormonal levels in normal men and in patients with benign prostatic hyperplasia. Eur Urol. 1991;20 Suppl 1:82-6.
7. http://bit.ly/IrgFYl (PDF)
8. Irwig, MS., Kolukula, S. Persistent sexual side effects of finasteride for male pattern hair loss. J Sex Med. 2011 Jun;8(6):1747-53.
9. Hamilton, J.B. Effect of castration in adolescent and young adult males upon further changes in the proportions of bare and hairy scalp. J Clin Endocrinol Metab. 1960 Oct;20:1309-18.
10. Dawber, R.P.P., et al. Disorders of hair. In: Champion RH, Burton JL, Durns DA (eds) Rook/Wilkinson/Ebling textbook of dermatology, 6th edn. Blackwell Science, Oxford, pp 2869–2973 1998
11. Olsen, E.A., et al. Androgenetic alopecia. In: Olsen EA (ed) Disorders of hair growth, diagnosis and treatment. McGraw-Hill, New York, pp 257–283 1994
12. Su, L.H. & Chen, T.H. Association of androgenetic alopecia with metabolic syndrome in men: a community-based survey. Br J Dermatol. 2010 Aug;163(2):371-7
13. González-González, J.G., et al. Androgenetic alopecia and insulin resistance in young men. Clin Endocrinol (Oxf). 2009 Oct;71(4):494-9.
14. Arias-Santiago, S., et al. Sex hormone-binding globulin and risk of hyperglycemia in patients with androgenetic alopecia. J Am Acad Dermatol. 2011 Jul;65(1):48-53.
15. Ahouansou, S., et al. Association of androgenetic alopecia and

hypertension. Eur J Dermatol. 2007 May-Jun;17(3):220-2. Epub 2007 May 4.

16. Arias-Santiago, S., et al. [Male androgenetic alopecia and cardiovascular risk factors: A case-control study]. Actas Dermosifiliogr. 2010 Apr;101(3):248-56.

17. Cela, E., et al. Prevalence of polycystic ovaries in women with androgenic alopecia. Eur J Endocrinol. 2003 Nov;149(5):439-42.

18. Starka, L., et al. Premature androgenic alopecia and insulin resistance. Male equivalent of polycystic ovary syndrome? Endocr Regul. 2005 Dec;39(4):127-31.

19. Lotufo, P.A., et al. Male pattern baldness and coronary heart disease: the Physicians' Health Study. Arch Intern Med. 2000 Jan 24;160(2):165-71.

20. Yassa, M., et al. Male pattern baldness and the risk of prostate cancer. Ann Oncol. 2011 Aug;22(8):1824-7

21. Birch, M.P., et al. Female pattern hair loss. Clin Exp Dermatol. 2002 Jul;27(5):383-88.

22. Hamilton, J.B. Effect of castration in adolescent and young adult males upon further changes in the proportions of bare and hairy scalp. J Clin Endocrinol Metab. 1960 Oct;20:1309-18.

23. Greenwald, A.E. [Oral contraceptives and alopecia]. Dermatol Iber Lat Am. 1970;12:29-36.

24. Lynfield, Y.L. Effect of pregnancy on the human hair cycle. J Invest Dermatol. 1960 Dec;35:323-7.

25. Venning, V.A., Dawber, R.P. Patterned androgenic alopecia in women. J Am Acad Dermatol. 1988 May;18(5 Pt 1):1073-7.

26. Price, V.H., et al. Histology and hormonal activity in senescent thinning in males. J Invest Dermatol. 2001;117:434.

27. Hamilton, J.B. Effect of castration in adolescent and young adult males upon further changes in the proportions of bare and hairy scalp. J Clin Endocrinol Metab. 1960 Oct;20:1309-18.

A SHIFT IN PARADIGM

"The cells in hair follicles produce hair when they are furnished
with everything they need. But in the scalp of a balding man,
they do not get everything they need and as a result, the hair-
producing cells gradually die off. Here we have an example of a
mild 'disease' which is caused by cellular malnutrition."
—Nobel laureate Dr. Roger J. Williams

In the last chapter I cast doubt on the two predominant
theories of pattern baldness: "bad genes" and "male"
hormones. Dr. Hamilton's research with eunuchs
demonstrated that while one may be susceptible to balding
due to his or her inherited physiological state, hair loss
would not manifest in the absence of environmental
influences – mainly, according to Hamilton, exposure to
testosterone. Three decades later, Dr. Julianne Imperato-
McGinley discovered that members of a group of
pseudohermaphrodites were immune to baldness and had
normal levels of testosterone, seemingly at odds with
Hamilton's theory that had implicated testosterone. The
pseudohermaphrodites were, however, deficient in the
enzyme that converts testosterone into
dihydrotestosterone (DHT), 5-alpha reductase. This
discovery was thought to provide a more specific

mechanism for baldness and helped to create the first FDA-approved drug for treating "male-pattern baldness" called Finasteride.

The findings of Dr. Hamilton and Dr. Imperato-McGinley, along with the partial effectiveness of Finasteride, helped form what is believed to be the strongest evidence for the cause of "androgenic alopecia", or "male-pattern baldness": "male" androgen hormones. However, because levels of the "male" hormones vary from person to person in pattern baldness, the theory needed a post hoc modification in order to reconcile this inconsistency; this modification came in the form of an inherited genetic sensitivity. While heavily relied upon to explain the mechanism of hair loss in young and middle-aged men, this inherited genetic sensitivity is completely jettisoned in other "types" of "male-pattern" baldness, including female androgenic alopecia, newborn hair loss, postpartum hair loss, menopausal hair loss and senescent alopecia, all of which are conveniently explained away as androgen-independent or age-related conditions. Additionally, some estimates suggest that androgenic alopecia affects 50 to 100 percent of White men and women, and to lesser degree minorities, an estimate that would require an improbably high rate of gene mutation.

Setting the androgen hypothesis aside, we find that baldness is incontrovertibly associated with aging, with research actually suggesting that premature baldness is a sign of premature aging.[1] An understanding of the mechanisms behind degeneration and regeneration would not only help to form a more coherent picture of pattern hair loss, but would also help to establish a context for devising effective and rational therapies for reversing it. The new context would need to reconcile the following observations: why balding occurs in both men and women, why balding is associated with aging, why castrates and pseudohermaphrodites are immune to baldness, and why drugs like Finasteride are effective for roughly half of those who use them.

The conclusions drawn in this book are unconventional, so before we go any further I urge you, the reader, to look back and reflect on whether I may have led you along a garden path. The remainder of this book is a radical departure from the current view of baldness and mechanistic physiology in general. While resources for those interested in pattern baldness are few and far between, Ralph M. Trüeb and Desmond Tobin's 2010 book, *Aging Hair*, provides, in my opinion, a relevant counter point to the ideas presented in this book. However, the future doesn't appear to be bright, as the two state:

> Mainly because the pathogenesis mechanisms of androgenic alopecia are not fully understood, the treatments available are limited and vary in effectiveness. Over the centuries a wide range of remedies have been suggested for androgenic alopecia and currently treatments include wigs and hairpieces, surgery, hormone action modifiers, and non-hormonal therapy. Several of these are based on our understanding of the mechanisms of androgen action within the follicle.

Hair Loss & Aging

The dominant theory of aging coursing through the veins of the medical world is the early 20th century biologist Raymond Pearl's "rate of living" theory of aging, which states that an organism's lifespan is inversely related to its basal metabolic rate, initially based on a previous observation that Drosophila melanogaster, a type of fly, lived longer when kept at a lower temperature than at a higher temperature.[2] Some have compared the body to a machine based on our everyday experience with them; that is, the more vigorously we use them, the faster they tend to wear out and malfunction. And if the body were indeed like a machine, it might seem reasonable to view a low pulse rate, low blood pressure, and a low body temperature as being "protective" or suggestive of longevity. Various nutritional and lifestyle "therapies" such as bathing in ice, fasting, and "trying not to burn too much glucose" (i.e., ketosis) are outgrowths of this thinking, and seem sensible as interventions in this context.

This concept runs counter to experiments done by the father of modern biochemistry, Nobel laureate Albert Szent-Györgyi, who demonstrated that tissue renewal was dependent on the energetic state of the organism. In his classic 1972 book, *The Living State*, Szent-Györgyi described a simple experiment in which the normal apparatus of excitation in a frog's heart was eliminated, making it solely dependent on electrical stimulation. When the electrical stimulation ceased, the experimenter expected to find a stronger heartbeat because of the resting period. Instead he found the opposite: the first beat after the pause was weaker, and became increasingly weaker as the pause got longer. The second beat, however, was stronger, as was each successive beat. Szent-Györgyi called this phenomenon "the staircase," explaining that function generates function, motion generates motion, while inactivity begets inactivity and makes motion and life fade away.

A real world example of Szent-Györgyi's "staircase" is evident in the incredible regenerative abilities of youth. In the 1998 book, *The Body Electric*, author Robert Beck describes how the high-energy, high-metabolic state of the youth is capable of repairing the most common childhood injury, the amputation of the fingertip. The standard medical treatment for a fingertip amputation entails smoothing out exposed bone and stitching the skin closed. If the digit has been cleanly cut, microsurgery is needed to reattach the fingertip. Despite these advanced methods, nails are deformed, fingers are too short and often the injury becomes a chronic source of pain. In the 1970s a child with such an injury benefitted from a hospital mix-up. While the physician dressed the wound, a referral to a surgical physician to close the wound was never made. Cynthia Illingworth caught the error a few days later, and to her amazement, the young rapscallion's fingertip was regenerating. Illingworth began treating other children with 'natural replacement' and by 1974 had documented several hundred regrown fingertips, all in children eleven years old or younger. Other clinical studies had confirmed that young children's fingers cleanly sheared off beyond the outermost crease of the outermost joint would invariably regrow perfectly in about three months.[3] When a probe was moved across the surface of the wounds of 10 children who had finger tip amputations, the currents recorded were remarkably similar to those obtained by Borgens et al. (1977) on salamanders, rising to a peak average current density of 22 mu A cm-2 after an average of 8 days.[4]

Given the extraordinary regenerative abilities demonstrated in children, why has more research not been devoted to optimizing the metabolic rate as a means to replicate this regenerative potential in adulthood? Perhaps mirroring the metabolism of a ten-year-old child would provide the same regenerative abilities that are common at that age.

The Stress of Aging

In 1947, Hungarian physiologist Hans Selye, who pioneered the stress concept of aging and disease, noted that prolonged or excessive exposure to a stressor would transiently lead to physiological imbalance, to which the body would mount an adaptive response so as to restore balance. However, the more numerous and severe the stressors became, the greater the physiological imbalance would result, and the likelihood of mounting an effective adaptive response would become progressively less likely.[5]

This mismatch – between the magnitude of the stressor and the adaptive response – would then lead to only a partial restoration of balance and excessive strain on the adaptive mechanisms. As these adaptive mechanisms began to fail, Selye saw a characteristic pattern of signs manifest that included hemorrhaging, shrinkage of the thymolymphatic tissue, inflammation and bleeding of the gastrointestinal tract, and enlargement of the adrenal cortex.

Although details of the science of stress is more speculative than concrete at this point, Selye made clear that the stressors encountered by an individual in his lifetime not only accelerate the aging process, but also damage the mechanisms that respond to those stressors. When subsequent stressors are encountered, the stress hormones are released in larger amounts and persist in the blood longer than they did in youth. The stress hormone cortisol was the focus of Selye's research, so I will use it as an example here to demonstrate my point. Normally, when a stressor is encountered, cortisol is secreted and shortly after cleared from the blood, operating on the principle of negative feedback, executed at the hypothalamus. But in old age, this negative feedback mechanism becomes less effective and allows cortisol to persist in the blood longer, presumably by damaging the cortisol "receptors" in the hypothalamus. Moreover, cortisol is secreted in larger amounts, pointing to the fact that the body has lost the ability to measure the amount of cortisol needed to deal with stressors, or that cortisol is acting less efficiently on its target tissues. Cortisol in excess is a destructive hormone, causing conditions as diverse as skin aging and muscle wasting to diabetes and cancer. Part of the way cortisol does this is by interfering with the proper delivery, use, and storage of glucose.

Selye (incorrectly) believed that every organism had a

finite amount of physiological reserve, or "adaptive energy," to mount an effective response to counteract the physiological disturbances caused by stressors of any kind. What's more likely happening is that the stress hormones an individual is exposed to in his lifetime cumulatively damage the mechanisms whereby the body responds to stressors, resulting in, foremost, an inefficiency of energy generation, as well as chronically elevated levels of the stress hormones. This not only accelerates the aging process, but contributes further to the malfunctioning of the body's stress response mechanisms. In an effort to keep us alive, these mechanisms are sustained at the expense of the whole body until balance, the main concern, is reestablished. But when we are no longer able to reestablish that balance, fragility and death are the inevitable outcomes.

The process of regeneration and the ability to avoid the ravages of stress correspond to the degree of metabolic intensity, and therefore the ability to sufficiently deliver glucose and oxygen to cells. Youth is associated with an uncanny ability to regenerate and a resiliency to stressors, whereas adulthood is deemed a declining state of imperfect repair and associated with an impaired ability to bounce back from those same stressors. The average rate of energy expenditure as a function of age can be represented as a U-shaped curve. The first few decades of life are characterized by high rates of energy expenditure, eventually hitting a plateau in middle age, and declining 1 to 2 percent per decade thereafter.[6]

The Energy-Stress Tug-o-War

In his 2001 book, *Life at the Cell and Below-Cell Level*, Dr. Gilbert Ling said, "Smiling, laughing and other normal physiological activities tell us that a baby is well. This is just a short way of saying that the trillions of cells making up the baby are well. Similarly, when the baby is sick, it is a short way of saying that some or all of the baby's cells are sick." While this might sound esoteric, Albert Szent-Györgyi (who called Ling one of the 'most inventive' biochemists he had ever met) wrote that a healthy cell needs energy not only for all of its functions, but to maintain its structure. In other words, the energy "flowing" through the cell (i.e., redox reactions and the cyclic "flow" of electrons) reinforces the cell's structure. When energy isn't being generated vigorously, the structure collapses.

Anything that interferes with the ability to generate sufficient quantities of energy necessarily interferes with the repair and renewal processes of cells, eventually leading to atrophy, infirmity, and complete loss of functioning of tissues and organs. In other words, a lack of energy has a "ripple-effect" throughout the entire organism, as cells form tissues, tissues form organs, and organs form whole organisms.

A complex "mini-organ", the hair follicles in people with pattern baldness show signs of maladaptation and stress – just like other aging organs do. Accordingly, refocusing attention on the interaction among stress, energy, and aging should help us to better understand the pathology underlying pattern baldness.

This leads to a Kubrick-esque mystery of what causes aging. While medical culture sees the organism as a ridged piece of non-renewable machinery preprogrammed with an inherited genetic destiny, Albert Szent-Györgyi, Hans Selye, Gilbert Ling, Ray Peat and others have described a very different 'energetic' view of life where an organism's structural resilience and ability to regenerate is based on its respiratory intensity – influenced predominantly by the environment. Focusing on the energetic state of the smallest unit of life, the cell, will lead us to discover an unexplored realm of science, the "flow" of energy through an organism (i.e., bioenergetics) and the mechanisms underlying the growth of hair, forming a heretical bioenergetic view of pattern hair loss.

References

1. Trüeb, R.M. Pharmacologic interventions in aging hair. Clin Interv Aging. 2006 June; 1(2): 121–129.
2. Loeb, J., and Northrop, J.H. Is There a Temperature Coefficient for the Duration of Life? Proc Natl Acad Sci U S A. 1916 Aug;2(8):456-7.
3. Illingworth, C.M. Trapped fingers and amputated finger tips in children. J Pediatr Surg. 1974 Dec;9(6):853-58.
4. Illingworth and Barker. Measurement of electrical currents emerging during the regeneration of amputated finger tips in children. 1980 Clin. Phys. Physiol. Meas. 1 87
5. H, S., et al. The legacy of Hans Selye and the origins of stress research: a retrospective 75 years after his landmark brief "letter" to the editor# of nature. Stress. 2012 Sep;15(5):472-8.
6. Speakman, J.R., et al. Living fast, dying when? The link between aging and energetics. J Nutr. 2002 Jun;132(6 Suppl 2):1583S-97S.

A BIOENERGETIC VIEW OF PATTERN BALDNESS

"He was started on thyroid therapy with the suggestion that after a time this should make him feel better, but there was little hope of recovering his hair. Two months later, when I saw him again, his depression had lifted, his blood pressure was down to normal, he was energetic, interested in life, and, to my own as well as his astonishment, hair was growing all over his head."
—Dr. Broda Barnes

In the last chapter, we showed that stress and deficient cellular energy are directly linked to both aging and baldness. We also learned that energy production becomes less efficient with age and that the adaptive "stress" hormones and signaling substances make up for this lost energy, with some people even suggesting that aging is caused by a maladaptation to stress. The provision of glucose and oxygen to cells determines our ability to generate energy and therefore our ability to tolerate the ravages of the stressors we encounter all day long. Because protein and fat can be converted to glucose, oxygen is the ultimate bottleneck in the ability to meet energy requirements by way of glucose oxidation.

In his 1957 book *Bioenergetics*, Nobel laureate Albert Szent-Györgyi wrote that if an organism's oxygen supply is periodically interfered with, the organism will slowly deteriorate, beginning with the loss of the ability to generate "efficient" or "youth-like" energy through the mitochondria. The interdependence of energy and structure, described by Albert Szent-Györgyi (and later by Raymond Peat, PhD) is seen in the efficiency by which energy is generated, with oxygen, in the mitochondria (technically called oxidative phosphorylation or mitochondrial respiration or oxidative metabolism). This process occurs in two phases: the anaerobic phase and the aerobic phase.

In the anaerobic phase (without oxygen), glucose (6 carbon atoms) is broken down into two pyruvate molecules (2 carbon atoms each) in the cell's cytoplasm. In the aerobic phase (with oxygen), the two pyruvate molecules generated in the anaerobic phase are decarboxylated (carbon dioxide removed) and have lipoic acid molecules attached to them yielding two molecules of acetyl-CoA. The acetyl-CoA molecules then enter the Krebs cycle in the mitochondria, producing small amounts of energy before realizing the complete oxidation of glucose in the electron transport chain, where almost all the energy that could possibly be derived from glucose is derived.

Cells without oxygen convert pyruvate to lactate, rather than acetyl-CoA, generating small amounts of energy in the process and allowing glycolysis to continue to 'run' in the absence of oxygen. This inefficient process, called glycolysis (or fermentation), not only generates many times less energy than oxidative metabolism does, but is also inflammatory. Lactate activates many mediators of inflammation, which are also incidentally involved in the genesis of baldness; in stark contrast, lactate does not accumulate during mitochondrial respiration but is instead removed from the blood.[1] Mitochondrial respiration is approximately 93 percent more efficient than fermentation[2] as far as energy is concerned; however, the advantage of the former process hinges largely on the "waste product" carbon dioxide.

Carbon dioxide allows cells, tissues, and organs to better absorb oxygen, essentially "breathing oxygen into us." The Danish physician Christian Bohr is credited for elucidating the details of this finding, showing in 1903 that carbon dioxide, produced by properly respiring cells, caused hemoglobin molecules (the proteins on which red blood cells bind and transport molecular oxygen) to release their oxygen atoms, increasing the availability of oxygen to cells (i.e., the Bohr effect). In this respect, carbon dioxide and lactate share an inverse relationship, evidenced by the fact that lactate levels are no higher during bouts of exertion as a person acclimates to a higher altitude, where oxygen levels are lower than they are at sea level. This phenomenon is called the lactate paradox. It indicates that at high altitude some sort of acclimatization occurs in which more carbon dioxide is retained in the tissues than is normal, such that the delivery of oxygen to tissues keeps up with demand, despite the fact that oxygen concentrations in the atmosphere are markedly reduced. If energy is generated without producing sufficient amounts of carbon dioxide, a situation similar to hyperventilation occurs, where large amounts of carbon dioxide are blown off through the lungs, which, in turn, leads to cellular hypoxia, despite the fact that normal amounts of oxygen are being carried by the blood.

This cyclical process hinges on the availability of active thyroid hormone or triiodothyronine (T3), which is predominantly synthesized in the liver from the "pro-hormone" thyroxine (T4). For the genesis of baldness, we are concerned with the active thyroid hormone's **dual role** as "**the hormone of respiration**"—stimulating oxygen consumption through the efficient breakdown of carbohydrates, fats, and proteins into carbon dioxide—and as a **cofactor** (along with cholesterol and vitamin A) in the production of the "youth-associated" steroid hormones (e.g., pregnenolone, progesterone and DHEA). Changes in hair growth, color and texture are famously associated with low thyroid function, which coincides with the age-associated decline in the production, transport, and activation of the thyroid hormones. Without the active thyroid hormone, and the corresponding respiratory efficiency that it provides, tissues would not function properly, leading to a laundry list of symptoms including weakness, dry skin, lethargy, slow speech, edema, sensation of cold, decreased sweating, thick tongue, pallor of skin, impaired memory, constipation, and mitochondrial dysfunction.

Oxygen, carbon dioxide, active thyroid hormone, and the vitality of the mitochondria form the foundation of our 'bioenergetic' view of pattern baldness. Since cells form tissues, tissues form organs, and organs form whole organisms, it follows as a matter of course that energy generated by cells, either "inefficiently" or "efficiently", has a "ripple effect" throughout the entire organism.

The hair follicle itself is a complicated mini-organ that stands to be negatively affected by even subtle shifts in the efficiency with which energy is generated. In fact, because of the already inherent inefficiency of metabolism present therein, the hair follicle is one of the most sensitive among all the organs to these shifts.

The Mini-Organ

Hair follicles are aggregates of cellular structures that produce hair in a highly energy-consuming process. However, when compared to a muscle cell, the energy metabolism in hair follicles can be characterized as "inefficient", converting proportionately more glucose to lactic acid,[3] which may explain why changes in hair growth and appearance manifest as quickly as they do during times of stress and malnutrition.

The vitality of the hair follicles is dependent on the health of the mitochondria, which require oxygen and glucose to produce sufficient energy in order to support this mitochondrial health. In 2013, Vidali et al. showed that hair follicle aging (graying, hair loss, etc.) correlated with declining mitochondrial function,[4] and by logical extension, lower energy levels. Dysfunctional mitochondria are not only thought to be a problem in hair loss, but practically all major illnesses including, but not limited to, Alzheimer's disease,[5] atherosclerosis,[6] autism,[7] cancer,[8] chronic fatigue,[9] fibromyalgia,[10] heart failure,[11] epilepsy,[12] hypertension,[13] hypoglycemia,[14] insulin resistance,[15] depression,[16] infertility,[17] migraine,[18] non-alcoholic liver disease,[19] obesity,[20] sleep apnea,[21] and type II diabetes.[22] While an allopathic doctor may be tempted to view each of these conditions differently, in 2007 Rodriguez, et al. noted that there were commonalities among all mitochondrial-based disorders:

1) Lower cellular ATP
2) Proportionately more reliance on fermentative energy (i.e., glucose to lactic acid)
3) Greater production of reactive oxygen species (ROS)[23]

Unfavorable changes in mitochondrial function can be traced back to the interference in either the production of thyroid hormone, transport of thyroid hormone, activation of thyroid hormone, or by any combination of these three processes. Thyroid hormone greatly affects mitochondrial health by stimulating the production of ATP, regulating oxygen consumption via carbon dioxide, and by reducing the production of reactive oxygen species.

Mechanisms of Pattern Hair Loss

Various adaptive "stress" substances that suppress thyroid function may explain the pathological changes seen in pattern baldness. For example, a characteristic of low thyroid is the accumulation of mucopolysaccharides – combinations of proteins and sugars that deposit in the area between cells called the extracellular space.[24] Evidence suggests that mucopolysaccharides, a hallmark of low thyroid, accumulate in the scalps of those men with pattern baldness and can act as a matrix for calcification.[25]

First published in 1942 in the prestigious Journal of the American Medical Association, the concept of increased scalp calcification in those with baldness is not new. In the publication, Dr. Frederick Hoelzel introduced his "ivory dome" theory of baldness based on observations he made in 1916 to 1917 while serving as a technician in gross anatomy at the College of Medicine of the University of Illinois. During that time he removed the brains of about 80 cadavers and discovered a correlation between the blood vessel supply to the scalp and the quantity of hair present. In the cadavers with baldness, blood vessels that nourished hair had been "pinched" off by excessive calcification in the cavities (foramen) of the skull bones through which these blood vessels passed, thereby impairing circulation to the scalp. Dr. Hoelzel concluded that "hair tonics" or vitamins were not likely to restore blood circulation, through blood vessels that had practically become impeded by "solid ivory".[26]

Dr. Hoelzel's theory has been met with extreme skepticism over the years, but there is ancillary evidence supporting the notion that pattern baldness is associated with reduced follicular blood flow. For example, when researchers compared balding vs. non-balding scalps, they found that balding scalps produced finer, less pigmented hairs that were much less obviously vascularized. However, when they exposed balding scalp cultures to a supplemental blood supply, the growth rate of the balding scalp cultures increased by about 80 to 90 percent.[27] In another study, biopsies of balding regions of scalp were accompanied by vascular thrombosis, the formation of a blood clot inside a blood vessel that obstructs the flow of blood and nutrients to the hair follicle. In the final stages of pattern baldness the tissue surrounding the hair follicle gradually lost their capillaries until the skin appeared to be almost deprived of blood vessels.[28] Similarly, reduced scalp oxygenation was noted by Goldman et al. in 1996, whose group stated that there was vascular insufficiency in regions of the scalp that lose hair during male pattern baldness.[29] Later on, Freund and Schwartz (2010) demonstrated that injections of botulinum toxin (i.e., botox) resulted in increased oxygen delivery to the frontal areas of the scalp, resulting in reduced hair loss and new hair growth among men with pattern baldness.[30]

In addition to the local changes seen in the scalps of those with pattern baldness, there are systemic changes that support Dr. Hoelzel's "ivory dome" theory of baldness. For example, it was found that bald men had reduced bone mineral density when compared to men with hair[31] and that balding was associated with several hormones that are not only uniquely detrimental to bones, but also to optimal thyroid function. By stimulating the production of carbon dioxide, the active thyroid hormone supports bone health. In point of fact, those with osteopetrosis or "marble-bone" disease have a deficiency of an enzyme that degrades carbon dioxide (carbonic anhydrase) and therefore have higher tissue levels of carbon dioxide. This leads to extremely strong "marble" bones, as carbon dioxide is a co-factor that directs calcium into teeth and bones and away from soft tissue.[32,33]

At the cell level, "inefficient" respiration (i.e., glucose to lactate) provides a viable mechanism for the higher functioning of adaptive "stress" hormones, poor bone mineral density, reduced follicular blood supply, scalp hypoxia, increased oxidative stress, and other unfavorable changes seen in pattern baldness. While these problems are traditionally viewed in a compartmentalized fashion, our bioenergetic view of the organism redirects our main focus to the mitochondria. The mitochondria need glucose and oxygen to produce energy, with oxygen being the ultimate "bottleneck" in "efficient" mitochondrial energy production. Regulating the availability of oxygen is the so-called "waste product" carbon dioxide, a product of oxidative metabolism, whose formation is empowered by the active thyroid hormone T3.

The following chapters provide evidence that several factors normally thought to be "protective" of hair actually contribute to baldness: estrogen, serotonin, and the "essential" fatty acids. These chapters will build on the bioenergetic context established in this chapter and the previous chapters. However, before we get too far, we need to re-review the work of Dr. Hamilton and Dr. Imperato-McGinley as well as the mechanism of action of Finasteride to explain why 100 percent of castrates and pseudohermaphrodites and roughly 40 percent of Finasteride users are immune to baldness.

References

1. Warburg, O., et al. Metabolism of Tumors in the Body. J Gen Physiol. 1927 March 7; 8(6): 519–530.
2. Lehninger, A. Bioenergetics: The Molecular Basis of Biological Energy Transformations. 1973
3. Adachi, K., et al. Human Hair Follicles: Metabolism and Control Mechanisms. J. Soc. Cosmet. Chem., 21, 901-924 (Dec. 9, 1970).
4. Vidali, S., et al. Hypothalamic-Pituitary-Thyroid Axis Hormones Stimulate Mitochondrial Function and Biogenesis in Human Hair Follicles. J Invest Dermatol. 2013 Jun 27.
5. Lucia, P., et al. Amyloid-Beta Interaction with Mitochondria. Int J Alzheimers Dis. 2011; 2011: 925050.
6. Nageswara, R., et al. Mitochondrial Dysfunction in Atherosclerosis. Circulation Research. 2007; 100: 460-473
7. Weissman, J.R., et al. Mitochondrial disease in autism spectrum disorder patients: a cohort analysis. PLoS One.

2008;3(11):e3815.

8. Balliet, R.M., et al. Mitochondrial oxidative stress in cancer-associated fibroblasts drives lactate production, promoting breast cancer tumor growth: understanding the aging and cancer connection. Cell Cycle. 2011 Dec 1;10(23):4065-73.

9. Myhill, S., et al. Chronic fatigue syndrome and mitochondrial dysfunction. Int J Clin Exp Med. 2009;2(1):1-16. Epub 2009 Jan 15.

10. Cordero, M.D., et al. Mitochondrial dysfunction and mitophagy activation in blood mononuclear cells of fibromyalgia patients: implications in the pathogenesis of the disease. Arthritis Res Ther. 2010;12(1):R17.

11. Huss J.M., and Kelly, D.P. Mitochondrial energy metabolism in heart failure: a question of balance. J Clin Invest. 2005 Mar;115(3):547-55.

12. Simon Waldbaum and Manisha Patel. Mitochondrial dysfunction and oxidative stress: a contributing link to acquired epilepsy? J Bioenerg Biomembr. 2010 December; 42(6): 449–455.

13. Puddu, P., et al. The putative role of mitochondrial dysfunction in hypertension. Clin Exp Hypertens. 2007 Oct;29(7):427-34.

14. Spiekerkoetter, U., and Wood, P.A. Mitochondrial fatty acid oxidation disorders: pathophysiological studies in mouse models. J Inherit Metab Dis. 2010 Oct;33(5):539-46.

15. Vial, G., et al. Liver mitochondria and insulin resistance. Acta Biochim Pol. 2010;57(4):389-92. Epub 2010 Nov 16.

16. Rezin, G.T., et al. Mitochondrial dysfunction and psychiatric disorders. Neurochem Res. 2009 Jun;34(6):1021-9.

17. Ramalho-Santos, J., et al. Mitochondrial functionality in reproduction: from gonads and gametes to embryos and embryonic stem cells. Hum Reprod Update. 2009 Sep-Oct;15(5):553-72.

18. Bigal, M.E., et al. New migraine preventive options: an update with pathophysiological considerations. Rev Hosp Clin Fac Med Sao Paulo. 2002 Nov-Dec;57(6):293-8. Epub 2003 Feb 17.

19. Wei, Y., et al. Nonalcoholic fatty liver disease and mitochondrial dysfunction. World J Gastroenterol. 2008 Jan 14;14(2):193-9.

20. Bournat, J.C., and Brown, C.W. Mitochondrial dysfunction in obesity. Curr Opin Endocrinol Diabetes Obes. 2010 Oct;17(5):446-52

21. Wang, Y., et al. Reactive oxygen species and the brain in sleep apnea. Respir Physiol Neurobiol. 2010 Dec 31;174(3):307-16.

22. Zhongmin, A.M., et al. Mitochondrial Dysfunction and β-Cell Failure in Type 2 Diabetes Mellitus. Exp Diabetes Res. 2012; 2012: 703538.

23. Rodriguez, M.C., et al. Beneficial effects of creatine, CoQ10, and lipoic acid in mitochondrial disorders. Muscle Nerve. 2007

Feb;35(2):235-42.

24. Crovato, F., et al. Histochemistry of Dermis and Blood Vessels in Male Pattern Alopecia. Biopathology of Pattern alopecia, pp. 191-199. Karger, Basel/New York 1968.

25. Johnson, W.C., and Helwig E.B. Histochemistry of the acid mucopolysaccharides of skin in normal and in certain pathologic conditions. Am J Clin Pathol. 1963 Aug;40:123-31.

26. Hoelzel, F. Baldness and Calcification of The "Ivory Dome". JAMA. 1942;119(12):968.

27. Randall, V.A., et al. A comparison of the culture and growth of dermal papilla cells from hair follicles from non-balding and balding (androgenetic alopecia) scalp. Br J Dermatol. 1996 Mar;134(3):437-44.

28. Crovato, F., et al. Histochemistry of Dermis and Blood Vessels in Male Pattern Alopecia. Biopathology of Pattern alopecia, pp. 191-199. Karger, Basel/New York 1968.

29. Goldman, B.E., et al. Transcutaneous PO2 of the scalp in male pattern baldness: a new piece to the puzzle. Plast Reconstr Surg. 1996 May;97(6):1109-16; discussion 1117.

30. Freund, B.J., and Schwartz, M. Treatment of male pattern baldness with botulinum toxin: a pilot study. Plast Reconstr Surg. 2010 Nov;126(5):246e-248e.

31. Morton, D.J., et al. Premature graying, balding, and low bone mineral density in older women and men: the Rancho Bernardo study. J Aging Health. 2007 Apr;19(2):275-85.

32. Bushinsky, D.A., et al. Metabolic, but not respiratory, acidosis increases bone PGE(2) levels and calcium release. Am J Physiol Renal Physiol. 2001 Dec;281(6):F1058-66.

33. Canzanello, V.J., et al. Effect of chronic respiratory acidosis on calcium metabolism in the rat. J Lab Clin Med. 1995 Jul;126(1):81-7.

A BIOENERGETIC VIEW OF ESTROGEN

"Several explanations for the beneficial effects of estrogens have been offered, but there are problems with most of them."
—Constance R. Martin, PhD

The last chapter solidified our bioenergetic concept of pattern baldness, noting that aging typically coincides with reduced energy expenditure and increases the reliance on the adaptive "stress" hormones that interfere with thyroid hormone production to promote "inefficient" cellular respiration. Over time, this leads to unfavorable changes in energy metabolism within hair follicles, degrading its structure. It also leads to pathological changes in the scalp tissue that can temporarily, or permanently, inhibit hair growth (e.g., inflammation, calcification, reduced follicular blood flow, hypoxia, oxidative stress).

However, this bioenergetic context doesn't directly address the evidence originally presented by Dr. Hamilton and Dr. Imperato-McGinley, who demonstrated that castrates and pseudohermaphrodites were immune to baldness in every single case studied. Similarly, the only FDA-approved treatment—with the possible side effect of permanent chemical castration—Finasteride, effective in roughly half of those individuals who take it, supposedly works by reducing the concentration of "male" hormones.

The idea of "gender" hormones (i.e., testosterone is the "male" hormone and estrogen is the "female" hormone) extends to other diseases including polycystic ovarian syndrome, prostate cancer, menopause and, most recently, the so-called andropause. However, when adopting a "whole organism view of physiology," hormone gender specificity becomes untenable. For example, testosterone can be converted to estrogen by an enzyme whose activity increases during stress, aging and malnutrition. Estrogen can also act on the adrenal glands, causing them to secrete an androgen responsible for causing whisker growth and chest hair.[1] While the concept of "male hormone" and "female hormone" makes it easier to sell drugs like Propecia, it makes little sense physiologically.

Perhaps the largest casualty of this medical reductionism is the physiological role of estrogen. Commonly believed only to support everything feminine, estrogen's negative influence on energy metabolism speaks to an alternative view of estrogen as an agent of stress, aging, and pattern baldness.

Estrogen: The Shock Hormone?

In 1947, pioneering endocrinologist Hans Selye discovered that estrogen mimicked the most severe state stress, shock. Rather than "producing estrus," (i.e., the female readiness to mate), administering estrogens to animals interrupted estrus and were actually "anti-estrogenic." Rejecting the name, Selye preferred to call estrogen "adipin", because of its production in the fat tissue (adipocytes), or "folliculin", because of the ovarian follicle's significant role in its production.[2] Today, however, estrogen has shed its identity as the "shock hormone", and has been ingrained into the cultural zeitgeist as the "female hormone" through a bizarre course of events.

In her 2005 essay, "The Rise and Fall of Estrogen Therapy: The History of HRT," Carla Rothenberg explains that over several decades, estrogen acquired a reputation as an antidote for many of the illnesses associated with aging, and even as a preventative drug for such diseases as osteoporosis, benign prostate hyperplasia (BPH), heart disease, and Alzheimer's disease. As part of a billion dollar business, estrogen "replacement" of 15 times the amount a young woman would produce normally has been embraced by doctors, drug manufacturers, and advertising agencies in a supposed effort to support femininity into old age. What could go wrong? After all, estrogen is "the female hormone" and scores of observational and case studies have supported an overwhelmingly positive view of replacing "lost" estrogen.

In 1991, the National Institutes of Health announced The Women's Health Initiative, a large clinical trial designed to test the effectiveness of various hormones and supplements compared to placebos. The largest study ever conducted of its kind, the trial involved a total of 161,808 healthy postmenopausal women. The morning of July 9, 2002, however, things went really wrong. A safety-monitoring board suddenly halted a part of the study involving 16,608 women because those women who were taking estrogen had more breast cancer, heart attacks, strokes, pulmonary embolisms, and blood clots than the women who were taking placebos. This was surprising to many physicians who were prescribing estrogen for the very illnesses estrogen was apparently causing; but if they had been aware of the effect of estrogen on cellular respiration, and if they had implemented a bioenergetic framework in the provision of care in their medical practice, it wouldn't have been.

Estrogen, Progesterone & Hair Growth

In women, estrogen is normally produced in monthly surges during ovulation or pregnancy, inducing a temporary loss of coherence within the organism. The monthly estrogen surge inhibits "efficient" oxidative mitochondrial metabolism and stimulates cell division.[3] In good health, this intense but brief stimulation is useful in situations that require rapid growth (i.e., for growing the uterus, breasts, and pituitary or for tissue repair following injury), but in other situations, can become degenerative if unopposed by large amounts of progesterone.

Progesterone acts as an anti-estrogen,[4,5] supporting oxidative mitochondrial respiration and resolving the temporary growth-state induced by estrogen. However, if the factors needed to produce progesterone – such as thyroid hormone and vitamin A – are deficient, as they typically are in advanced age, estrogen can accumulate in the tissues to lower the metabolic rate and the efficiency by which energy is generated. The anti-respiratory, pro-inflammatory nature of estrogen, a systemic problem, has many anti-hair qualities.

One of the clearest examples of how estrogen and progesterone affect hair growth is during pregnancy, when there is an increase in hair growth rate, hair diameter, and ratio of growing hairs to resting hairs[6,7] – all of which result in a "lush head of hair."[8] In fact, in some cases pregnancy reverses "male-pattern" baldness in women.[9] In contrast to the beneficial effects of pregnancy on hair growth, postpartum women routinely experience dramatic hair loss.[10] But after giving birth, when progesterone levels fall sharply and estrogen and prolactin (the "lactation" or "molting hormone") levels increase,[11] the lush head of hair that had developed during pregnancy – when progesterone levels were soaring – disappears.

In stark contrast to the hair-supportive conditions of pregnancy, menopausal conditions favor the development of "male-pattern baldness".[12] While professionals often proclaim menopause as an "estrogen deficiency"—as if there were no doubt about it—it is very clear, instead, that an elevated ratio of estrogen to progesterone is involved. Estrogen concentrations in tissues correlate positively with aging[13,14,15] and with body fat levels.[16,17] Because there is much misunderstanding, it is worth stating here that blood levels of estrogen do not necessarily reflect tissue concentrations of estrogen.[18,19,20,21] Increased by estrogen,[22,23] prolactin often becomes excessive around menopause,[24] slows the metabolic rate,[25] and inhibits the production of progesterone.[26]

However, there is no denying that supplemental estrogen is sometimes "helpful" during menopause, but this may be due estrogen's suppression of the pituitary "menopausal" gonadotropins, which in excess can cause many problems associated with menopause. In fact, P.W. Wise found that regulatory nerves in the brain responsible for releasing these "menopausal" hormones were "desensitized" in relation to their exposure to estrogen.[27,28]

Estrogen and prolactin tend to cause hair loss in animals too. In one study, administering estrogen to rodents caused hair loss, while an antiestrogen drug renewed hair growth.[29] In another experiment, dogs treated with large doses of estrogens lost their coats, which persisted even after the experiment ended.[30] Similarly, prolactin treated rodents experience hair loss,[31] and both estrogen and prolactin work together to initiate molting in birds.[32]

The influence of pregnancy, post-pregnancy and menopause on hair growth has now been elucidated by the bioenergetic properties of estrogen, prolactin and progesterone: Estrogen and prolactin both suppress thyroid function[33] and interfere with the "efficient" production of energy,[34,35] while progesterone opposes both hormones[36] and supports respiration.[37] Not surprisingly, estrogen and prolactin were increased in those with pattern

48

baldness.[38,39]

Estrogen, Prolactin & Osteoporosis

Estrogen's "anti-hair" "anti-respiratory" qualities are further supported by what is considered its greatest strength: its effect on bone health. Estrogen is said to help prevent osteoporosis by decreasing the production of cells that destroy bone called osteoclasts. While estrogen does slow osteoclast production, it also decreases the rate of bone renewal and promotes the deposition of calcium in soft tissue.

Perhaps the most striking anti-bone quality of estrogen is that it stimulates the secretion of the pituitary hormone prolactin.[40,41] A well-known function of prolactin is to break down bone to provide calcium for milk production during lactation. Unsurprisingly, lactating mothers are at very high risk for osteoporosis,[42] as well as other ailments that include depression and hair loss. A hormone that tends to increase with prolactin (and vice versa) and also removes calcium from the bones is parathyroid hormone (PTH).[43] While the increased secretion of parathyroid hormone is adaptive in the short-term (normalizing blood calcium levels when they fall below normal), low levels of parathyroid hormone are essential for maintaining bone health.[44] Consistent with its role in causing errant calcification processes, parathyroid hormone has also been shown to influence hair growth in animal experiments.[45]

Estrogen, prolactin, and parathyroid hormone tend to suppress thyroid function, reducing the concentration of carbon dioxide, promoting "inefficient" respiratory energy, the production of lactic acid, all of which lead to an increased reliance on the classical stress hormone cortisol. Cortisol, secreted from the adrenal glands during stress, degrades the body's proteins before turning them into glucose so as to quickly provide large amounts of glucose to cells to deal with the stressors. When energy metabolism is inhibited, as it is in diabetes,[46] cortisol rises despite high blood glucose levels. Because the exposure to cortisol is increased in age-related bone loss[47] and in pattern-baldness,[48] cortisol is thought to at least contribute to those conditions.

Progesterone's opposition towards estrogen, prolactin, cortisol, and parathyroid hormone helps clarify the complex relationships among the endocrine factors involved in bone loss. This same biochemical web, in context, also allows for a reevaluation of the original research presented by Dr. Hamilton and Dr. Imperato-McGinley, explaining why castration and pseudohermaphrodites were immune to baldness all of the time, without exception. And finally, this context offers an alternative hypothesis for how the popular anti-androgen drug Finasteride works.

Revisiting The Androgen Hypothesis

Let's revisit Dr. Hamilton's 1942 research, focusing on the three anomalies found in those with testicular insufficiency:

1) Absence of balding
2) A marked reduction in sebaceous gland activity, resulting in reduced oiliness of the face, hair, and scalp, as well as an absence of acne
3) Dandruff that was either present in very small amounts or absent altogether.

Acne, dandruff, and general oiliness of the skin are thought to be, at least in part, caused by increased sebaceous gland activity. Because we know that castrates do not produce testosterone (with the exception of small amounts of testosterone and other weaker androgens from the adrenal glands), it might seem reasonable to treat these problems with anti-androgens; in practice, however, this approach has produced mixed results.[49]

When analyzing the hormones of a castrate, we find that, in addition to the absence of testosterone, castrates are also deficient in estrogen[50] and prolactin.[51] These hormones influence sebaceous glands;[52] in particular, prolactin activates the formation of sebum (oil) by the skin. Lo and behold, the anti-prolactin drug Bromocriptine has been successfully used to treat acne.[53] Vitamin A opposes the action of estrogen and is commonly used to treat acne.[54] Aspirin not only reduces estrogen,[55] but, like the other inhibitors of eicosanoid synthesis (e.g., zileuton), is also useful in situations involving acne.

A hormonal anomaly unifying Hamilton's castrates[56] and Dr. Imperato McGinley's pseudohermaphrodites[57] is the "higher functioning" of the pituitary gonadotropin, luteinizing hormone (LH), which stimulates the ovaries to secrete progesterone in women, the testes to secrete testosterone in men, and the adrenal glands to secrete androgens in both men and women. While progesterone levels were not measured in either case, the castrates and pseudohermaphrodites exhibited feminized characteristics (e.g., reduced beard growth, higher pitched voices, and reduced pubic hair growth), all but confirming the notion that the groups had either higher than normal levels of progesterone, an anti-androgen, or unusually low levels of estrogen in relation to the adrenal androgens and progesterone, as the estrogens can be masculinizing.[58] (The castrates were probably deficient in the enzymes that convert the adrenal androgens and progesterone to testosterone and estrogen.)

Similarly, Finasteride may have progesterone-like qualities. Chemically similar to progesterone, Finasteride is helpful for the types of hair loss that are arbitrarily deemed to be "androgen independent". For instance, in a study of eight females with normal levels of androgens, Finasteride arrested the progression of hair loss for half of the women who used it.[59] Another piece of evidence showing that

Finasteride has progesterone-like qualities came in the form of an observation that younger men respond better to Finasteride than older men do.[60] Because estrogen tends to accumulate with aging at the same time testosterone, an anti-estrogen, declines,[61] the "estrogenized" aging male may have more difficulty experiencing the full force of Finasteride's feminizing effects, provided Finasteride did, in fact, have progesterone-like qualities. According to its most recent package insert, Finasteride is so potently feminizing in some males that it has been shown to induce breast development, reduce beard growth, and eliminate libido[62] – all confirming Finasteride's progestogenic qualities.

Anything but the "female hormone", estrogen is involved in the genesis of stress, aging, and pattern baldness. Its effects on hair growth are most clearly seen in pregnancy and menopause. During pregnancy progesterone, which opposes estrogen, increases roughly 100 times more than normal, often resulting in a "lush head of hair" and reversing so-called female androgenic alopecia. During lactation, when progesterone levels fall, and prolactin, estrogen, and cortisol increase, postpartum mothers notoriously experience hair loss that is often considered excessive. Similarly, during menopause—also an estrogen dominant state—women often experience "male-pattern baldness". Changes in hair growth during pregnancy and menopause are further elucidated by these hormones' influence on energy metabolism. For example, estrogen and prolactin promote the energetically inefficient non-oxidative metabolism, while progesterone supports the creation of thyroid hormones and, therefore, the energetically efficient oxidative metabolism. So, it's all but fair to suppose that because an interference in energy metabolism induces temporary hair loss, when estrogen and prolactin are activated chronically, pathological changes in the scalp develop, ultimately leading to permanent pattern baldness by way of hypoxia, soft tissue calcification, poor blood flow, nutrient loss, oxidative stress, and so forth.

References

1. Ditkoff, E.C., et al. The impact of estrogen on adrenal androgen sensitivity and secretion in polycystic ovary syndrome. J Clin Endocrinol Metab. 1995 Feb;80(2):603-7.
2. Selye, H. The Textbook of Endocrinology. 1947. "Similarly, in many animal species, the so-called "estrogens" do not in themselves cause estrus or heat without simultaneous progesterone treatment, hence the later hormone could be called 'estrogenic' with almost equal justification. Furthermore, folliculoids interrupt the estrous cycle in the intact rodent so that they are actually 'anti-estrogenic' under ordinary circumstances of bioassay."
3. Gross, M. Biochemical changes in the reproductive cycle. Fertil Steril. 1961 May-Jun;12:245-62.
4. Liu, J.W., et al. Estrogen replacement in ovariectomized rats results in physiologically significant levels of circulating progesterone, and co-administration of progesterone markedly reduces the circulating estrogen. Endocrine. 1997 Apr;6(2):125-31.
5. Pasqualini, J.R., et al. The anti-aromatase effect of progesterone and of its natural metabolites 20alpha- and 5alpha-dihydroprogesterone in the MCF-7aro breast cancer cell line. Anticancer Res. 2008 Jul-Aug;28(4B):2129-33.
6. Muallem, M.M., and Rubeiz N.G. Physiological and biological skin changes in pregnancy. Clin Dermatol. 2006 Mar-Apr;24(2):80-3.
7. Nissimov, J., and Elchalal, U. Scalp hair diameter increases during pregnancy. Clin Exp Dermatol. 2003 Sep;28(5):525-30.
8. Clarence R. Robbins. Morphological, Macromolecular Structure and Hair Growth. Chemical and Physical Behavior of Human Hair. 2012, pp 1-104.
9. Behrman, H.T. The Scalp in Health and Disease. p. 101 St. Louis, the C.v. Mosby Company, 1952
10. Lynfield Y.L. Effect of pregnancy on the human hair cycle. J Invest Dermatol. 1960 Dec;35:323-7.
11. Randall, V.A. and Botchkareva, N.V. The Biology of Hair Growth. Centre of Skin Sciences, School of Life Scien
12. Venning, V.A., and Dawber, R.P. Patterned androgenic alopecia in women. J Am Acad Dermatol. 1988 May;18(5 Pt 1):1073-7.
13. Musey, V.C., et al. Age-related changes in the female hormonal environment during reproductive life. Am J Obstet Gynecol.

1987 Aug;157(2):312-7.

14. Wilshire, G.B., et al. Diminished function of the somatotropic axis in older reproductive-aged women. J Clin Endocrinol Metab. 1995 Feb;80(2):608-13.

15. Pirke KM, Doerr P. Age related changes in free plasma testosterone, dihydrotestosterone and oestradiol. Acta Endocrinol (Copenh). 1975 Sep;80(1):171-8.

16. Deslypere, J.P., et al. Fat tissue: a steroid reservoir and site of steroid metabolism. J Clin Endocrinol Metab. 1985 Sep;61(3):564-70.

17. Jensen, J., et al. The effects of age and body composition on circulating serum oestrogens and androstenedione after the menopause. Br J Obstet Gynaecol. 1985 Mar;92(3):260-5.

18. Batra, S., et al. Interrelations between plasma and tissue concentrations of 17 beta-oestradiol and progesterone during human pregnancy. Clin Endocrinol (Oxf). 1979 Dec;11(6):603-10.

19. Thijssen, J.H., et al. Uptake and concentration of steroid hormones in mammary tissues. Ann N Y Acad Sci. 1986;464:106-16.

20. Vermeulen-Meiners, C., et al. The endogenous concentration of estradiol and estrone in normal human postmenopausal endometrium. J Steroid Biochem. 1984 Nov;21(5):607-12.

21. Jefcoate, C.R., et al. Tissue-specific synthesis and oxidative metabolism of estrogens. J Natl Cancer Inst Monogr. 2000;(27):95-112.

22. D'Agata, R., et al. Hydrotestolactone lowers serum oestradiol and PRL levels in normal men: evidence of a role of oestradiol in prl secretion. Clin Endocrinol (Oxf). 1982 Nov;17(5):495-9.

23. Nicoletti, I., et al. Testosterone-induced hyperprolactinaemia in a patient with a disturbance of hypothalamo-pituitary regulation. Acta Endocrinol (Copenh). 1984 Feb;105(2):167-72.

24. Metka, M., et al. The role of prolactin in the menopause. Maturitas. 1994 Dec;20(2-3):151-4.

25. Strizhkov, V.V. [Metabolism of thyroid gland cells as affected by prolactin and emotional-physical stress]. Probl Endokrinol (Mosk). 1991 Sep-Oct;37(5):54-8.

26. Tulchinsky, D., and Little A.B. Maternal-Fetal Endocrinology, 2nd edn. Philadelphia, Saunders, 1994

27. Wise, P. M., "Influence of estrogen on aging of the central nervous system: Its role in declining female reproductive functions" in Menopause: Evaluation, Treatment, and Health Concerns, pages 53-70, 1989.

28. Wise, P.M., et al. "Neuroendocrine influences on aging of the female reproductive system," Frontiers in Neuroendocrinology 12, 323-356, 1991.

29. Oh H.S., and Smart R.C. An estrogen receptor pathway regulates the telogen-anagen hair follicle transition and influences

epidermal cell proliferation. Proc Natl Acad Sci U S A. 1996 Oct 29;93(22):12525-30.

30. Gardner, W.U., and DeVita, J. Inhibition of Hair Growth in Dogs Receiving Estrogens. Yale J Biol Med. 1940 December; 13(2): 213–215.

31. Langan, E.A., et al. Mind the (gender) gap: does prolactin exert gender and/or site-specific effects on the human hair follicle? J Invest Dermatol. 2010 Mar;130(3):886-91.

32. General Endocrinology. Saunders 1966.

33. Strizhkov, V.V. [Metabolism of thyroid gland cells as affected by prolactin and emotional-physical stress]. Probl Endokrinol (Mosk). 1991 Sep-Oct;37(5):54-8.

34. Gross, M. Biochemical changes in the reproductive cycle. Fertil Steril. 1961 May-Jun;12:245-62.

35. Strizhkov, V.V. [Metabolism of thyroid gland cells as affected by prolactin and emotional-physical stress]. Probl Endokrinol (Mosk). 1991 Sep-Oct;37(5):54-8.

36. Pasqualini, J.R., et al. The anti-aromatase effect of progesterone and of its natural metabolites 20alpha- and 5alpha-dihydroprogesterone in the MCF-7aro breast cancer cell line. Anticancer Res. 2008 Jul-Aug;28(4B):2129-33.

37. Gonzalez Deniselle, M.C., et al. Basis of progesterone protection in spinal cord neurodegeneration. J Steroid Biochem Mol Biol. 2002 Dec;83(1-5):199-209.

38. Schmidt, J.B., et al. Hormonal parameters in androgenetic hair loss in the male. Dermatologica. 1991;182(4):214-7.

39. Schmidt J.B., et al.[Hyperprolactinemia and hypophyseal hypothyroidism as cofactors in hirsutism and androgen-induced alopecia in women]. Hautarzt. 1991 Mar;42(3):168-72.

40. D'Agata, R., et al. Hydrotestolactone lowers serum oestradiol and PRL levels in normal men: evidence of a role of oestradiol in prl secretion. Clin Endocrinol (Oxf). 1982 Nov;17(5):495-9.

41. Nicoletti, I., et al. Testosterone-induced hyperprolactinaemia in a patient with a disturbance of hypothalamo-pituitary regulation. Acta Endocrinol (Copenh). 1984 Feb;105(2):167-72.

42. Kovacs, C.S. Calcium and bone metabolism during pregnancy and lactation. J Mammary Gland Biol Neoplasia. 2005 Apr;10(2):105-18.

43. Raymond, J.P., et al. Comparison between the plasma concentrations of prolactin and parathyroid hormone in normal subjects and in patients with hyperparathyroidism or hyperprolactinemia. J Clin Endocrinol Metab. 1982 Dec;55(6):1222-5.

44. Martin, C. Endocrine Physiology. 1985.

45. Safer, J.D., et al. A topical parathyroid hormone/parathyroid hormone-related peptide receptor antagonist stimulates hair

growth in mice. Endocrinology. 2007 Mar;148(3):1167-70. Epub 2006 Dec 14.

46. Alberti, L., et al. Type 2 diabetes and metabolic syndrome are associated with increased expression of 11beta-hydroxysteroid dehydrogenase 1 in obese subjects. Int J Obes (Lond). 2007 Dec;31(12):1826-31. Epub 2007 Jun 26.

47. Deuschle, M., et al. Effects of major depression, aging and gender upon calculated diurnal free plasma cortisol concentrations: a re-evaluation study. Stress. 1998 Dec;2(4):281-7.

48. Schmidt, J.B. Hormonal basis of male and female androgenic alopecia: clinical relevance. Skin Pharmacol. 1994;7(1-2):61-6.

49. Leyden, J., et al. A systemic type I 5 alpha-reductase inhibitor is ineffective in the treatment of acne vulgaris. J Am Acad Dermatol. 2004 Mar;50(3):443-7.

50. Selye, H. The Textbook of Endocrinology. 1976;661 "Eunuchism decreases urinary testoid 17-KS and folliculoid elimination, since it removes one of the most important sources of these compounds. The continued excretion, in small amounts, of such steroids in castrates, is probably attributable to adrenal-cortical secretion."

51. Bronson, F. Mammalian Reproductive Biology. 1991;63 "As expected then, castration is followed by a dramatic increase in the frequency of LH pulses and thus a much higher level of LH in the blood. In contrast, blood levels of prolactin fall after castration."

52. Zouboulis, C.C. Acne and sebaceous gland function. Clin Dermatol. 2004 Sep-Oct;22(5):360-6.

53. Peserico, A., et al. Bromocriptine treatment in patients with late onset acne and idiopathic hyperprolactinemia. Acta Derm Venereol. 1988;68(1):83-4.

54. BO, W.J. Relation of vitamin A deficiency and estrogen to induction of keratinizing metaplasia in the uterus of the rat. Am J Clin Nutr. 1957 Nov-Dec;5(6):666-73.

55. Hudson, A.G., et al. Nonsteroidal anti-inflammatory drug use and serum total estradiol in postmenopausal women. Cancer Epidemiol Biomarkers Prev. 2008 Mar;17(3):680-7.

56. Martin C. Endocrine Physiology. 1976:533 "Plasma FSH and luteinizing hormone (LH) levels rise after castration."

57. Imperato-McGinley, J., et al. Luteinizing hormone pulsatility in subjects with 5-alpha-reductase deficiency and decreased dihydrotestosterone production. J Clin Endocrinol Metab. 1994 Apr;78(4):916-21.

58. Ditkoff, E.C., et al. The impact of estrogen on adrenal androgen sensitivity and secretion in polycystic ovary syndrome. J Clin Endocrinol Metab. 1995 Feb;80(2):603-7.

59. Moreno-Ramírez. D., and Camacho Martínez, F. Frontal fibrosing

alopecia: a survey in 16 patients. J Eur Acad Dermatol Venereol. 2005 Nov;19(6):700-5.

60. Camacho, F.M., et al. Value of hormonal levels in patients with male androgenetic alopecia treated with finasteride: better response in patients under 26 years old. Br J Dermatol. 2008 May;158(5):1121-4. Epub 2008 Mar 20.

61. Vermeulen, A,. et al. Testosterone secretion and metabolism in male senescence. J Clin Endocrinol Metab. 1972 Apr;34(4):730-5.

62. http://bit.ly/1hh8nRY (PDF)

A BIOENERGETIC VIEW OF
SEROTONIN

"A theory that is wrong is considered preferable to admitting our
ignorance."
—Elliot Vallenstein, PhD

A recent health article discussed the negative side effects
of a short-lived pharmaceutical drug for irritable bowel
syndrome called Zelnorm. Taking Zelnorm resulted in a
ridiculous amount of side effects, including abdominal
pain, chest pain, flushing, facial edema, hypertension,
hypotension, angina pectoris, syncope, arrhythmia, anxiety,
vertigo, ovarian cyst, miscarriage, menorrhagia,
cholecystitis, appendicitis, bilirubinemia, gastroenteritis,
increased creatine phosphokinase, back pain, cramps,
breast cancer, attempted suicide, impaired concentration,
increased appetite, sleep disorder, depression, anxiety,
asthma, increased sweating, renal pain, polyuria, heart
attacks, and intestinal ischemia/necrosis. The author
explained that the mechanism of the drug was that it
"acted like serotonin," concluded that it had some serious
problems, and should be avoided at all costs. Instead, he

preferred to use tryptophan or 5-HTP (i.e., serotonin precursors) in patients with poor intestinal health.

This clear-cut case of cognitive dissonance supports the strong cultural stereotype of serotonin as the "happy chemical that can do no wrong." However, in our bioenergetic, context, serotonin sheds its cultural identity and shows itself for what it truly is: a chemical involved in the genesis of stress, aging and pattern baldness.

Depression, Stress & Energy

Although it is stated with great confidence that depression involves low levels of serotonin, it's never been definitively proven in humans that a deficiency of serotonin causes depression.[1] Serotonin reuptake inhibitors (SSRIs), which prolong the effects of serotonin in the brain, among other places, are about as effective as a placebo.[2] Accumulating cases of children, teens, and young adults (ages 18 to 24) committing suicide and developing suicidal thinking patterns have even led the FDA to force drug manufacturers to add a black box warning – the most serious of all warnings – to all the drugs in the SSRI class, warning prescribers, pharmacists, and patients of this very serious risk.[3] However, some people find great relief with these antidepressants, but that may have nothing to do with serotonin per se, as serotonin increases the adaptive "stress" hormone, cortisol[4,5,6] that can result in a sense of "extraordinary wellbeing and buoyancy" followed by "mood swings" and "suicidal tendencies".[7,8]

I propose that a "higher functioning" of serotonin is probably involved in the pathology of depression. Depression is the result of energy problems, the ones I've been describing, exacerbated by all the things that interfere with energy generation, including an excessive exposure to serotonin. Thyroid hormone and aspirin (salicylic acid) stimulate uncoupling of the mitochondria, thereby increasing oxygen consumption, carbon dioxide production,[9] and heat generation. In short, all the things associated with efficient oxidative metabolism. Is it then any wonder that the supplementation of thyroid hormone and aspirin has been shown to help alleviate depression?[10,11,12] Lo and behold, drugs that lower serotonin, serotonin-reuptake enhancers (SSREs), are effective agents for depression.[13,14]

Studies have helped to elucidate and confirm the anti-metabolic effects of serotonin. One study found that serotonin induced swelling in the mitochondria, and that adenosine triphosphate (ATP) reversed that swelling demonstrating that serotonin and ATP act in opposing directions in the cell.[15] Another study found that serotonin interrupts oxidative mitochondrial respiration, promoting non-oxidative metabolism, increasing the formation of (the proinflammatory) lactic acid.[16] In agreement with the implications that could be logically drawn from these two studies, serotonin was shown to reduce ATP levels in the cell.

In animals, serotonin appears to be crucially involved in the transition to the hibernation state.[17] Serotonin slows the respiratory rate by increasing the activity of the enzyme (carbonic anhydrase) that degrades carbon dioxide.[18] On the other hand, administering thyroid hormone to hibernating animals wakes them up.[19]

Serotonin & Hair Growth

Serotonin's inhibition of "efficient" energy metabolism has adverse effects on the mini-organ known as the hair follicle. Like all tissues, the hair follicle is composed of collection of cells and depends on the "flow" of energy to function. Thyroid hormones regulate this process, controlling hair follicle energy metabolism as well as mitochondrial function. As we saw in the hibernating animals, serotonin shares an inverse relationship with the thyroid hormones. For example, individuals with low thyroid tend to have higher levels of serotonin.[20,21,22] Carbon dioxide, produced under the direction of the thyroid hormones, stabilizes circulating mast cells, preventing them from releasing their serotonin into the blood.[23]

In addition to its inverse relationship with the thyroid hormones, serotonin increases and synergizes with a variety of hormones associated with baldness. It, for instance, increases estrogen[24,25,26] (and estrogen, in turn, increases serotonin).[27] It, like estrogen, also increases prolactin.[28] And, it inhibits the formation of the pro-hair hormone progesterone.[29]

Increased prolactin is a typical side effect of SSRIs[30] and serotonin precursor supplements (such as 5-HTP and tryptophan), sometimes inducing gynecomastia (i.e., male breast growth) in men. Like estrogen and prolactin, serotonin causes bone loss and inhibits bone formation;[31] on this basis, anti-serotonin drugs have been used to inhibit bone loss.[32,33] Bone health is of particular interest given that the factors in bone health usually intersect with the factors in hair health (e.g., carbon dioxide, thyroid, estrogen, prolactin, parathyroid hormone, etc.).

Serotonin & Bacterial Endotoxin

A factor in stress, aging, and pattern hair loss that has yet to be mentioned is endotoxin, or lipopolysaccharide (LPS), which is a toxic, outer-cell wall component of certain bacteria that, like estrogen, produces shock and interferes with cells' use of oxygen.[34] This hair loss factor is normally produced by common colonic bacteria and released into the surrounding area upon their destruction or death. In stress, de-energized intestinal cells (enterocytes) become more promiscuous in the substances that they allow to enter the body, including endotoxin, which, upon slipping past this intestinal firewall, gets into the general circulation, through which it does almost all of its damage to the host.

Endotoxin synergizes with and increases many of the bioenergetic factors contributing to pattern baldness, especially serotonin. While often referred to as a brain neurotransmitter, the intestines produce about 95 percent of the body's serotonin,[35] whose basic function is to produce intestinal contractions. (This is probably why the producers of Zelnorm believed that it was a rational treatment of irritable bowel syndrome). Endotoxin causes the release of serotonin.[36] Serotonin, in turn, causes inflammation in the intestines[37] and appears in excess in inflammatory bowel diseases, such as irritable bowel syndrome (IBS), celiac disease, and Crohn's disease.[38]

Endotoxin also interacts with two other factors in baldness, cortisol and estrogen. Cortisol increases blood levels of endotoxin in a dose-dependent fashion,[39] and endotoxin activates the enzyme that synthesizes new estrogen.[40] In a vicious cycle, estrogen increases cortisol[41] and causes intestinal cells to become permeable.[42] Constipation, which was one of the earliest signs of stress noticed by Hans Selye,[43] increases estrogen, too.[44,45]

In context, serotonin—in its role as an inhibitor of the metabolic rate—seems to be a contributor to the pathology of pattern baldness. Serotonin's synergy with estrogen, prolactin, cortisol and endotoxin further elucidates its mechanism in the advent of hair loss. The evidence provided suggests a rethinking of a substance that is subject to as much bias and misinformation as the topic of our previous chapter, estrogen.

Our bioenergetic view of estrogen and serotonin can now establishes a foundation for reviewing what is perhaps the largest factor in our bioenergetic view of pattern baldness: the types of fat we consume. While dietary fat has been a focal point in nutrition research for the last several decades, the so-called deleterious fat, saturated fat, as part of the 'diet-heart-hypothesis', has been vindicated by the forward thinking pioneers like Dr. Chris Masterjohn, Uffe Ravnskov and others. Solving the riddle of pattern baldness may require a similar pioneering attitude towards the role of fatty acids in stress, aging and pattern hair loss. More specifically, the case will be made that the current darling of the nutrition industry, the polyunsaturated fats (including omega-3s) are uniquely harmful for hair growth, and may even be a prerequisite for pattern baldness.

References

1. Lacasse, J.R., and Leo, J. Serotonin and Depression: A Disconnect between the Advertisements and the Scientific Literature. PLoS Med. 2005 December; 2(12): e392.
2. Moncrieff, J., and Kirsch, I. Efficacy of antidepressants in adults. BMJ. 2005 July 16; 331(7509): 155–157.
3. http://1.usa.gov/1ayvYIE (PDF)
4. Lefebvre, H., et al. Serotonin-induced stimulation of cortisol secretion from human adrenocortical tissue is mediated through activation of a serotonin4 receptor subtype. Neuroscience. 1992;47(4):999-1007.
5. Neckers, L, Sze. Regulation of 5-hydroxytryptamine metabolism in mouse brain by adrenal glucocorticoids. Brain Res 1975 Jul 25;93(1):123-32.
6. Martin, C. Endocrine Physiology. 1985. "Serotonin acts centrally to affect renin release, and it promotes ACTH secretion."
7. Selye, H. The Story of Adaptation Syndrome. 1952. "Adaptive hormones can cause mental changes in man. Many patients who take ACTH or COL first develop a sense of extraordinary wellbeing and buoyancy, with excitement and insomnia; this is sometimes followed by a depression which may go so far as to create suicidal tendencies."
8. Martin, C. Endocrine Physiology. 1985. "Glucocorticoids exert early influences on the brain that tend to elevate mood and increase the sense of 'well-being.' Larger amounts can bring on temporary euphoria. However, the secondary effects include psychic depression. Patients with chronically elevated levels tend to have mood swings. They have been known to display bizarre behavior and to suffer hallucinations."
9. Bayram, E., et al. In vitro inhibition of salicylic acid derivatives on human cytosolic carbonic anhydrase isozymes I and II. Bioorg Med Chem. 2008 Oct 15;16(20):9101-5.

10. Ketterer, M.W., et al. Is aspirin, as used for antithrombosis, an emotion-modulating agent? J Psychosom Res. 1996 Jan;40(1):53-8.

11. Cooper, R., and Lerer, B. [The use of thyroid hormones in the treatment of depression]. Harefuah. 2010 Aug;149(8):529-34, 550, 549.

12. Andrade, N.E., et al. [Depression and anxiety symptoms in hypothyroid women]. Rev Bras Ginecol Obstet. 2010 Jul;32(7):321-6.

13. Wilde, M.I., et al. Tianeptine. A review of its pharmacodynamic and pharmacokinetic properties, and therapeutic efficacy in depression and coexisting anxiety and depression. Drugs. 1995 Mar;49(3):411-39.

14. Kasper, S., and McEwen B.S. Neurobiological and clinical effects of the antidepressant tianeptine. CNS Drugs. 2008;22(1):15-26.

15. Watanabe Y, Shibata S, Kobayashi B. Serotonin-induced swelling of rat liver mitochondria. Endocrinol Jpn. 1969 Feb;16(1):133-47.

16. Koren-Schwartzer, N., et al. Serotonin-induced decrease in brain ATP, stimulation of brain anaerobic glycolysis and elevation of plasma hemoglobin; the protective action of calmodulin antagonists. Gen Pharmacol. 1994 Oct;25(6):1257-62

17. Popova, N.K., et al. Involvement of brain tryptophan hydroxylase in the mechanism of hibernation. Pharmacol Biochem Behav. 1993 Sep;46(1):9-13.

18. Vullo, D., et al. Carbonic anhydrase activators: activation of the human isoforms VII (cytosolic) and XIV (transmembrane) with amino acids and amines. Bioorg Med Chem Lett. 2007 Aug 1;17(15):4107-12. Epub 2007 May 21.

19. Selye H. The Textbook of Endocrinology. 1947 "During hibernation, in such animals as the hamster, squirrel, etc. the thyroid undergoes profound atrophy, comparable in severity to that caused by hypophysectomy. The resulting decrease in thyroid-hormone production is essential for winter-sleep, since thyroid hormone administration awakens animals from this condition."

20. Henley, W.N., and Koehnle, T.J. Thyroid hormones and the treatment of depression: an examination of basic hormonal actions in the mature mammalian brain. Synapse 1997 Sep;27(1):36-44.

21. Henley, W.N., and Vladic, F. Hypothyroid-induced changes in autonomic control have a central serotonergic component. Am J Physiol 1997 Feb;272(2 Pt 2):H894-903.

22. Schwark WS, Keesey RR. Thyroid hormone control of serotonin in developing rat brain. Res Commun Chem Pathol Pharmacol. 1975 Jan;10(1):37-50.

23. Strider, J.W., et al. Treatment of mast cells with carbon dioxide

suppresses degranulation via a novel mechanism involving repression of increased intracellular calcium levels. Allergy. 2011 Mar;66(3):341-50.

24. Donner, N., et al. Estrogen receptor beta regulates the expression of tryptophan-hydroxylase 2 mRNA within serotonergic neurons of the rat dorsal raphe nuclei. Neuroscience. 2009 Oct 6;163(2):705-18. Epub 2009 Jun 23.

25. Hiroi, R., et al. Estrogen selectively increases tryptophan hydroxylase-2 mRNA expression in distinct subregions of rat midbrain raphe nucleus: association between gene expression and anxiety behavior in the open field. Biol Psychiatry. 2006 Aug 1;60(3):288-95. Epub 2006 Feb 3.

26. Bethea, C.L., et al. Steroid regulation of tryptophan hydroxylase protein in the dorsal raphe of macaques. Biol Psychiatry. 2000 Mar 15;47(6):562-76.

27. Berman, N.E., et al. Serotonin in trigeminal ganglia of female rodents: relevance to menstrual migraine. Headache. 2006 Sep;46(8):1230-45.

28. Clemens, J.A., et al. Further evidence that serotonin is a neurotransmitter involved in the control of prolactin secretion. Endocrinology. 1977 Mar;100(3):692-8.

29. Schaeffer H.J., and Sirotkin A.V. Melatonin and serotonin regulate the release of insulin-like growth factor-I, oxytocin and progesterone by cultured human granulosa cells. Exp Clin Endocrinol Diabetes. 1997;105(2):109-12.

30. Torre, D.L., et al. Pharmacological causes of hyperprolactinemia. Ther Clin Risk Manag. 2007 Oct;3(5):929-51.

31. Damsa, C., et al. "Dopamine-dependent" side effects of selective serotonin reuptake inhibitors: a clinical review. J Clin Psychiatry. 2004 Aug;65(8):1064-8.

32. Yadav, V.K., et al. Inhibition of gut-derived serotonin synthesis: a potential bone anabolic treatment. Nat Med, 16(3), pp. 308-312.

33. Inose, H., et al. Efficacy of serotonin inhibition in mouse models of bone loss. J Bone Miner Res. 2011 Sep;26(9):2002-11.

34. Lee-Ellen, C., et al. Pathophysiology, 4e. 2009

35. Martin, C. Endocrine Physiology. 1985. "Approximately 98% of total serotonin is found outside of the central nervous system. The blood platelets and gastrointestinal tract account for around 95% and serotonin is a component of both central and peripheral mast cells."

36. Davis, R.b., et al. Serotonin release by bacterial endotoxin. Proc Soc Exp Biol Med. 1961 Dec;108:774-6.

37. Bischoff, S.C., Role of serotonin in intestinal inflammation: knockout of serotonin reuptake transporter exacerbates 2,4,6-trinitrobenzene sulfonic acid colitis in mice. Am J Physiol Gastrointest Liver Physiol. 2009

38. Spiller, R. Serotonin, inflammation, and IBS: fitting the jigsaw together? J Pediatr Gastroenterol Nutr. 2007 Dec;45 Suppl 2:S115-9.

39. Mullington, J., et al. Dose-dependent effects of endotoxin on human sleep. Am J Physiol Regul Integr Comp Physiol. 2000 Apr;278(4):R947-55.

40. Christeff, N. et al. Effect of the aromatase inhibitor, 4 hydroxyandrostenedione, on the endotoxin-induced changes in steroid hormones in male rats. Life Sci. 1992;50(19):1459-68.

41. Caticha, O., et al. Estradiol stimulates cortisol production by adrenal cells in estrogen-dependent primary adrenocortical nodular dysplasia. J Clin Endocrinol Metab. 1993 Aug;77(2):494-7.

42. Enomoto, N., et al. Estriol sensitizes rat Kupffer cells via gut-derived endotoxin. Am J Physiol. 1999 Sep;277(3 Pt 1):G671-7.

43. Selye, H. The Stress of Life. 1978. "The gastrointestinal tract is particularly sensitive to general stress. Loss of appetite is one of the first symptoms in the great 'syndrome of just being sick,' and this may be accompanied by vomiting, diarrhea, or constipation."

44. Lewis, S.J., et al. Lower serum oestrogen concentrations associated with faster intestinal transit. Br J Cancer. 1997;76(3):395-400.

45. Lewis, S.J., et al. Intestinal absorption of oestrogen: the effect of altering transit-time. Eur J Gastroenterol Hepatol. 1998 Jan;10(1):33-9.

A BIOENERGETIC VIEW OF THE "ESSENTIAL FATTY ACIDS"

"Everyone should have the privilege of playing Russian Roulette if it is desired, but it is only fair to have the warning that with the use of polyunsaturated fats the gun probably contains live ammunition."
—Dr. Broda Barnes

Recently, it was found that men with "androgenic alopecia" had higher levels of the polyunsaturated fatty acid breakdown product, prostaglandin D2 (PGD2) in their scalps.[1] Naturally, this created a tidal wave in the hair loss community, lighting various forums ablaze with thread titles such as, "Hope for us all - Source of baldness discovered: Prostaglandin D2", "How can I reduce prostaglandin D2 to save my hair?" and "Prostaglandin inhibitor to cure baldness in two years!"

While the hair-loss-o-sphere was confused and excited at the same time, elevated levels of PGD2 in the scalps of balding men is to be expected given our bioenergetic context of hair loss. However, the current doctrine of the "essentiality" of certain fats has muddied the waters of baldness research, effectively handicapping progressive thought on the subject. Therefore, the role of the various types of dietary fats in human health, and by extension balding, demands a reimagining; a reimagining that turns the current ideas on the topic, including the current darling of the nutritional world – the polyunsaturated fats – on its head.

Dietary Fats 101

Although all fats and oils, whether of vegetable or plant origin, contain a mixture of saturated, monounsaturated, and polyunsaturated fats, they differ in the proportions of each of these fats; that is to say, the main difference is a matter of degree, not kind. Highly unsaturated fats (polyunsaturated fats, or PUFA) have more carbon double bonds and are more susceptible to spontaneous oxidation, while saturated fats have fewer double bonds and more hydrogen atoms, making them less susceptible to errant oxidation processes. While oxidation in the context of mitochondrial oxidative metabolism is beneficial and desired, unsaturated fats that react with oxygen-derived free radicals lead to oxidative stress to produce the conditions that favor the generation of the previously mentioned PUFA breakdown products, the prostaglandins, that, in one way or another, irreversibly damage the mitochondria.

In nature, we find that PUFA is appropriate for animals preparing for hibernation or living in cold climates, such as sardines in the ice-cold waters of the arctic. If we were to exchange the high concentration of PUFA in the tissue of sardines for an equally high concentration of saturated fatty acids, as is found in warm-blooded animals, those sardines would become stiff and unable to maneuver in the cold water. Likewise, a higher concentration of PUFA in warm-blooded animals would increase the fat's likelihood of oxidizing because of the higher temperatures, as well as the higher oxygen concentrations, present therein. Plants, nuts and seeds are the most concentrated sources of PUFA, whose degree of saturation depends on the climate in which the plants are grown. For instance, soybeans grown in tropical climates have the same degree of saturation that coconuts do.[2]

Humans have a high rate of metabolism and a body that operates optimally at a temperature around 98.6 degrees Fahrenheit, suggesting that saturated fats – which are stable against relatively high concentrations of oxygen and used exclusively to generate heat – are more appropriate for humans than unsaturated fats are.

However, the 1970s birthed the poorly substantiated "lipid hypothesis" and a medical doctrine which put forth the idea that saturated fats were responsible for heart disease, polluting lipid research for the next several decades. The cultural response to the lipid hypothesis was to minimize the consumption of saturated fats in favor of the cheap "heart healthy" refined oils (e.g., soybean oil, corn oil, cottonseed oil, vegetable oil, rapeseed oil, peanut oil, sesame oil, canola oil, etc.). In particular, it was estimated that the consumption of soybean oil has gone up 1000% in the last decade.[3] Rather than preventing heart disease, the increased consumption of unsaturated fats has coincided with the rapid decline of U.S. health, some even hypothesizing that the promotion of unsaturated fats have been partially responsible for the obesity epidemic.[4] While the topic continues to baffle the mainstream, Uffe Ravnskov, Dr. Chris Masterjohn and others have thoroughly picked apart the flaws in the "the lipid hypothesis," vindicating saturated fats in the process (for many of the same reasons that are discussed in this chapter).

Even more controversial than the role of unsaturated and saturated fats in human physiology is the role of the so-called "essential fatty acids," or EFAs, which include

- Omega-6 linoleic acid (LA)

- Omega-6 arachidonic acid (AA)
- Omega-3 alpha-linolenic acid (ALA)
- Omega-3 docosahexaenoic acid (DHA)
- Omega-3 eicosapentaenoic acid (EPA)

Found predominantly in oily fish such as salmon, halibut, and sardines, and in dietary supplements derived therefrom (e.g., fish oil, cod liver oil, salmon oil, krill oil), these fats, now universally believed to be beneficial, have been elevated to the status of vitamins. Especially when viewed in our bioenergetic context, however, the early research that deemed certain polyunsaturated fatty acids as "essential" seems, in my estimation, to have been presumptuous.

A Brief History of EFAs

The idea that some fats were essential began in 1929 when George and Mildred Burr published a paper claiming that a variety of diseases including dandruff, dermatitis, slowed growth, sterility, and fatal kidney degeneration were cured when their rodents were supplied with adequate linoleic acid (LA).[5] The experimental diet used to support this finding consisted of purified casein (a milk protein) and purified sucrose, aligned with supplemental vitamins and minerals. Besides being deficient in several nutrients that hadn't been discovered yet (e.g., zinc, copper, manganese, molybdenum, and selenium) the fat-deficient high-sucrose diet caused the rats to consume oxygen at an extremely high rate (i.e., increase their metabolic rates). Some wondered if rather than a deficiency of LA, the rats' nutritional requirements were simply higher due to their higher rates of metabolism. The suspicions of these few skeptical individuals were proven to be justified when the purported essential fatty acids deficiency was cured with the addition of vitamin B6,[6] suggesting that rather than curing a deficiency, the addition of LA was simply decreasing the rate of metabolism and therefore the nutritional requirements.

Interestingly, inducing an EFA deficiency in humans is rather difficult to do, as the Burr's discovered when their coworker William Brown agreed to adhere to an EFA-deficient diet for six months.[7] Brown's diet was limited to skimmed milk, skimmed cottage cheese, sucrose, potato starch, orange juice, baking powder, salt, and a few dietary supplements. Rather than "fat-free," the diet was extremely low fat, with most of the fat coming from the skimmed milk. The results of the six-month experiment found Brown in good health, indicated by the elimination of his weekly migraines and a reduced sense of fatigue after a day's work. The diet also reduced Brown's blood pressure, serum phosphorous levels, and weight, and increased his respiratory quotient (i.e., the oxidation of carbohydrate to carbon dioxide in relation to fat and protein). Additionally, Brown's blood cholesterol levels dropped from 298 to 206 mg/dL, while his serum triglycerides, the form in which fatty acids are safely trafficked throughout the body, increased.

In all, Brown's health actually improved dramatically on an EFA-deficient diet. These results coincide with other experiments that later demonstrated the anti-inflammatory and anti-stress effects brought about by an EFA deficiency. One mechanism that could explain the benefits of becoming EFA deficient is the synthesis of a polyunsaturated omega-9 fatty acid called mead acid, which a person produces in amounts proportional to the severity of his or her EFA deficiency.[8] Unlike other unsaturated fats, mead acid is anti-inflammatory,[9,10] supports mitochondrial respiration,[11,12] and protects against shock,[13] energy loss, and endotoxin.[14]

Insulin Resistance & Baldness

In September 2000, researchers raised the question of

whether insulin resistance was a mechanism or promoting factor in early pattern baldness.[15] Early on, insulin resistance is characterized by high blood levels of insulin, a 'compensation' for the resistance to insulin that develops in the body. Later on, when insulin secretion begins to fall off, high blood glucose levels (hyperglycemia) develops, and a diagnosis of type II diabetes is made.

Excess carbohydrate consumption is often thought to cause or greatly exacerbate these issues, and some have suggested that limiting our overall intake of carbohydrates, especially of sugar, would greatly ameliorate these problems.

Rather than excess carbohydrate, however, the preponderance of evidence suggests that excess fat, by elevating free fatty acids (non-esterified fatty acids or NEFA), causes insulin resistance.[16] The accumulation of free fatty acids in the blood can be thought of as a condition brought about by stress (any kind), executed by way of the adaptive "stress" hormones.[17] These stress hormones are all "lipolytic"—meaning that they liberate fatty acids into the blood. Adrenaline, cortisol, estrogen, growth hormone, and aldosterone (among others), inhibit the use of glucose in various tissues in order to spare that glucose for certain areas of the brain and the muscles as means to supply energy to power short bursts of explosive activity. While "burning fat" has become synonymous with meaningless diet jargon, Wolfe and his colleagues noted that "the enhanced mobilization and oxidation of fat is a fundamental response to stress," and that there was "little doubt that there are signals for the increased mobilization of fat [present] in shock, trauma, and sepsis."[18]

Free fatty acids interfere with energy metabolism in both the short-term and the long-term. In the short-term fatty acid metabolism inhibits the uptake and oxidation of glucose, as the British biochemist Sir Phillip Randle's hypothesis states.[19] In the long-term, free fatty acids have been referred to as a "toxic candidate" for the insulin-secreting pancreatic beta cells.[20] In fact, it was found that chronic exposure to even moderate amounts of fatty acids dysregulates and impairs the functioning of the beta cells, even destroying them in severe cases.[21] In contrast to the beta cell destroying effect of fatty acids, glucose has been shown to initiate the regeneration of beta cells, thereby restoring the physiological proportion of insulin secretion to glucagon secretion by the pancreas. For example, experiments with animals showed that infusions of glucose increased the mass of beta cells by 250 percent over the course of 4 days.[22] By reducing the cell's exposure to free fatty acids, glucose, by way of insulin, actually protects the mitochondria from harm.

Unsaturated fatty acids are specifically detrimental to energy production by interfering with oxygen use. Raymond Peat, PhD has brought attention to cardiolipin, a unique (double) phospholipid found exclusively in the mitochondria. In physical proximity, cardiolipin supports the activity of cytochrome c oxidase, an enzyme that occupies the last crucial step in the process of energy generation by way of oxidative phosphorylation. The fatty acid composition of cardiolipin changes with aging, "specifically [by] an increase in highly unsaturated fatty acids,"[23] and these changes decrease the activity of cytochrome c oxidase.

Perhaps the largest contribution of free fatty acids to the genesis of pattern baldness is their degradation into hormone-like inflammatory substances called prostaglandins. **While the common belief is that there are both "good" and "bad" prostaglandins, in the context of baldness they seem to be exclusively bad**. In stress, the cyclooxygenase (COX) enzymes are activated, metabolizing the "essential" fat arachidonic acid into prostaglandins. One of these prostaglandins, prostaglandin E2, activates aromatase,[24] increasing estrogen, which is associated with pattern baldness.[25] In a vicious cycle, estrogen activates the fat-liberating enzyme (phospholipase A2) that releases arachidonic from cells allowing prostaglandins to form.[26,27] Although correlational data cannot be magically turned into proof of cause and effect, balding men were found to have accumulated higher levels of prostaglandin D2 in their scalps, an observation that supports the body of evidence and mechanisms implicating COX, arachidonic acid, and prostaglandins in pattern baldness. Estrogen,[28,29,30,31] arachidonic acid,[32] and prostaglandins all stimulate the synthesis of prolactin, which is also associated with pattern baldness.[33]

In addition to inhibiting glucose metabolism, the efficiency of which is central to hair growth, elevated levels of free fatty acids have two well-defined negative effects on hormonal metabolism. The first is that free fatty acids, especially when unsaturated, facilitate the entry of estrogen into cells, possibly by lowering levels of sex hormone binding globulin (SHBG),[34,35] whose function is to bind and keep estrogen out of cells and in the blood. Lower levels of SHBG are associated with pattern baldness.[36,37,38] The second is that free fatty acids increase the activity of the rate-limiting enzyme (tryptophan hydroxylase) of the pathway that converts tryptophan to serotonin.[39] While this is considered to be beneficial by the rest of the world, as described in the last chapter, serotonin is a factor in pattern baldness that should be tightly regulated.

Before closing this chapter, it is important to bear in mind that overeating that leads to weight gain represents a stressor that can lead to chronically elevated levels of the free fatty acids. When energy intake exceeds energy requirements, over time, adipose tissue becomes overstuffed with fat and as a result, fatty acids leak out from the adipose tissue and into the blood, thereby raising the levels of free fatty acids. At the same time, the overstuffed adipose tissues increase the body's overall inflammatory burden, which, in a positive feedback loop, liberate even more fatty acids from the adipose tissue.

Although all free fatty acids, saturated or unsaturated, are harmful in excess, when they are saturated, the positive feedback loop just described would short circuit itself, as saturated fatty acids suppress the body's adaptive responses to stressors[40] and are quickly burnt to counteract the hypercaloric imbalance. But when the liberated fatty acids are unsaturated, as is undoubtedly now the case in those who eat the standard American, PUFA-laden diet, there is no such off switch as there is for saturated fatty acids, as unsaturated fatty acids interfere with the creation, release, transport, and activation of the thyroid hormone. Unsaturated fatty acids also irreversibly damage the mitochondria, increase estrogen and prolactin, and perpetuate the body's inflammatory state.

References

1. Garza, L.A., et al. Prostaglandin d2 inhibits hair growth and is elevated in bald scalp of men with androgenetic alopecia. Sci Transl Med. 2012 Mar 21;4(126):126ra34.

2. Wolf, R.B., et al. Effect of temperature on soybean seed constituents: Oil, protein, moisture, fatty acids, amino acids and sugars. Journal of the American Oil Chemists' Society May 1982, Volume 59, Issue 5, pp 230-232

3. Tanya, L.B., et al. Changes in consumption of omega-3 and omega-6 fatty acids in the United States during the 20th century. Am J Clin Nutr. 2011 May; 93(5): 950–962.

4. Ailhaud, G., et al. Temporal changes in dietary fats: role of n-6 polyunsaturated fatty acids in excessive adipose tissue development and relationship to obesity. Prog Lipid Res. 2006 May;45(3):203-36. Epub 2006 Feb 10.

5. Burr, G.O., and Burr, M.M. A new deficiency disease produced by the rigid exclusion of fat from the diet. J. Biol. Chem. 1929, 82:345-367.

6. Witten, P.W., and Holman, R.T. Polyethenoid fatty acid metabolism. VI. Effect of pyridoxine on essential fatty acid conversions. Arch Biochem Biophys. Dec 1952;41(2):266-273.

7. Brown, W.R., et al. Effects of prolonged use of extremely low-fat diet on an adult human subject.1942; 16(6):511-523.

8. Cleland, L.G., et al. Dietary (n-9) eicosatrienoic acid from a cultured fungus inhibits leukotriene B4 synthesis in rats and the effect is

modified by dietary linoleic acid. J Nutr. 1996 Jun;126(6):1534-40.

9. Lefkowith, J.B., et al. Manipulation of the acute inflammatory response by dietary polyunsaturated fatty acid modulation. J Immunol. 1990 Sep 1;145(5):1523-9.

10. Cleland, L.G., et al. Dietary (n-9) eicosatrienoic acid from a cultured fungus inhibits leukotriene B4 synthesis in rats and the effect is modified by dietary linoleic acid. J Nutr. 1996 Jun;126(6):1534-40.

11. Burr, G.O., and Beber, A.J. Metabolism Studies With Eats Suffering From Fat Deficiency. Exp Biol Med May 1934 vol. 31 no. 8 911-912

12. Kunkel, H., and Williams, J. The effects of fat deficiency upon enzyme activity in the rat. J Biol Chem. 1951 Apr;189(2):755-61.

13. Cook, J.A., et al. Essential fatty acid deficient rats: a new model for evaluating arachidonate metabolism in shock. Adv Shock Res. 1981;6:93-105.

14. Li, E.J., et al. Resistance of essential fatty acid-deficient rats to endotoxin-induced increases in vascular permeability. Circ Shock. 1990 Jun;31(2):159-70.

15. Matilainen, V., et al. Early androgenetic alopecia as a marker of insulin resistance. Lancet. 2000 Sep 30;356(9236):1165-6.

16. M Roden, T.B., et al. Mechanism of free fatty acid-induced insulin resistance in humans. J Clin Invest. 1996 June 15; 97(12): 2859–2865.

17. Frayn, K.N., et al. Are increased plasma non-esterified fatty acid concentrations a risk marker for coronary heart disease and other chronic diseases? Clin Sci (Lond). 1996 Apr;90(4):243-53.

18. Wolfe, R.R., et al. Energy metabolism in trauma and sepsis: the role of fat. Prog Clin Biol Res. 1983;111:89-109.

19. Hue, L., and Taegtmeyer, H. The Randle cycle revisited: a new head for an old hat. Am J Physiol Endocrinol Metab. 2009 Sep;297(3):E578-91.

20. Li N, Frigerio F, Maechler P. The sensitivity of pancreatic beta-cells to mitochondrial injuries triggered by lipotoxicity and oxidative stress. Biochem Soc Trans. 2008 Oct;36(Pt 5):930-4.

21. Piro, S., et al. Chronic exposure to free fatty acids or high glucose induces apoptosis in rat pancreatic islets: possible role of oxidative stress. Metabolism. 2002 Oct;51(10):1340-7.

22. Jetton, T.L., et al. Enhanced beta-cell mass without increased proliferation following chronic mild glucose infusion. Am J Physiol Endocrinol Metab. 2008 Apr;294(4):E679-87.

23. Lee, H.J., et al. Selective remodeling of cardiolipin fatty acids in the aged rat heart. Lipids Health Dis. 2006 Jan 23;5:2.

24. Bulun, S.E., et al. Estrogen biosynthesis in endometriosis: molecular basis and clinical relevance. J Mol Endocrinol. 2000

Aug;25(1):35-42.

25. Schmidt, J.B., et al. Hormonal parameters in androgenetic hair loss in the male. Dermatologica. 1991;182(4):214-7.

26. Thomas, W., et al. Estrogen induces phospholipase A2 activation through ERK1/2 to mobilize intracellular calcium in MCF-7 cells. Steroids. 2006 Mar;71(3):256-65. Epub 2005 Dec 22.

27. Periwal, S.B., et al. Effect of hormones and antihormones on phospholipase A2 activity in human endometrial stromal cells. Prostaglandins. 1996 Mar;51(3):191-201.

28. D'Agata, R., et al. Hydrotestolactone lowers serum oestradiol and PRL levels in normal men: evidence of a role of oestradiol in prl secretion. Clin Endocrinol (Oxf). 1982 Nov;17(5):495-9.

29. Nicoletti, I., et al. Testosterone-induced hyperprolactinaemia in a patient with a disturbance of hypothalamo-pituitary regulation. Acta Endocrinol (Copenh). 1984 Feb;105(2):167-72.

30. Horner, K.C., et al. Experimental estrogen-induced hyperprolactinemia results in bone-related hearing loss in the guinea pig. Am J Physiol Endocrinol Metab 293: E1224–E1232, 2007.

31. Matsuda, M., and Mori, T. Effect of estrogen on hyperprolactinemia-induced glucose intolerance in SHN mice. Proc Soc Exp Biol Med. 1996 Jul;212(3):243-7.

32. Kolesnick, R.N., et al. Arachidonic acid mobilizes calcium and stimulates prolactin secretion from GH3 cells. Am J Physiol. 1984 May;246(5 Pt 1):E458-62.

33. Schmidt, J.B., et al.[Hyperprolactinemia and hypophyseal hypothyroidism as cofactors in hirsutism and androgen-induced alopecia in women]. Hautarzt. 1991 Mar;42(3):168-72.

34. Reed, M.J., et al. Free fatty acids: a possible regulator of the available oestradiol fractions in plasma. J Steroid Biochem 1986 Feb;24(2):657-659.

35. Bruning, P.F., and Bonfrèr, J.M. Free fatty acid concentrations correlated with the available fraction of estradiol in human plasma. Cancer Res. 1986 May;46(5):2606-9.

36. Arias-Santiago, S., et al. Sex hormone-binding globulin and risk of hyperglycemia in patients with androgenetic alopecia. J Am Acad Dermatol. 2011 Apr 19.

37. Starka, L., et al. [Hormonal profile in men with premature androgenic alopecia]. Sb Lek. 2000;101(1):17-22.

38. Cipriani, R., Sex hormone-binding globulin and saliva testosterone levels in men with androgenetic alopecia. Br J Dermatol. 1983 Sep;109(3):249-52.

39. McNamara, R.K, et al. Omega-3 fatty acid deficiency during perinatal development increases serotonin turnover in the prefrontal cortex and decreases midbrain tryptophan hydroxylase-2 expression in adult female rats: dissociation from

estrogenic effects. J Psychiatr Res. 2009 Mar;43(6):656-63. Epub 2008 Nov 4.

40. Katoh, K., et al. Saturated fatty acids suppress adrenocorticotropic hormone (ACTH) release from rat anterior pituitary cells in vitro. Comp Biochem Physiol A Mol Integr Physiol. 2004 Feb;137(2):357-64.

STEPS TOWARD A LOGICAL "PRO-HAIR" LIFESTYLE

"It's refreshing to see people beginning to think clearly and rationally and move away from gimmicky diets that have little basis in fact, reality, or objectivity, and to ones that are firmly seated in all aspects of human physiology and science. After all, this is why most of us choose to eat a certain way, that is to be as healthy as we can be, both physically and mentally . . . not to, say, replicate how our caveman ancestors supposedly ate and lived. It's due to this line of reasoning that carbohydrates, and especially sugar and fructose, have fallen by the wayside of late, driven by an irrational fear, bordering on obsessiveness, that's evolved to where sugar is now conceived of as a toxic poison and blamed for causing diabetes, cancer, obesity, gout, etc. (Thank you Dr. Lustig.)"
—Andrew Kim

Pattern baldness is an energy problem that begins in the cell. Solving that energy problem involves limiting our exposure to adaptive "stress" substances such as cortisol, estrogen, prolactin, serotonin, endotoxin, parathyroid hormone and aldosterone. Our ability to defend against these adaptive "stress" substances depends on our ability to sufficiently deliver oxygen and glucose to our cells.

Because carbohydrate, protein, and fat can provide glucose, oxygen is the ultimate bottleneck in the "efficient" production of energy through the mitochondria. Oxygen is regulated in large by thyroid hormones, and more specifically, active thyroid hormone, triiodothyronine (T3), which is produced predominantly in the liver from the "pro-hormone" thyroxine (T4).

Thyroid hormones regulate the rate of oxygen consumption in two ways; by stimulating the production of carbon dioxide and acting as a cofactor in the synthesis of various "youth-associated" hormones (e.g., pregnenolone, progesterone, DHEA). Thus, a lifestyle that supports hair growth can also be thought of as an "anti-stress" or "pro-thyroid" lifestyle. While it may sound far-fetched to influence how our cells produce energy, there are many environmental factors that affect the creation, transport, and activation of the thyroid hormones.

The Importance of Self-Diagnostics

Before we get into the dietary and lifestyle suggestions, it's imperative that you, the reader, be aware of self-diagnostics that should be employed during any dietary and lifestyle endeavor. Adopting an arbitrary list of dietary recommendations without collecting objective data is a waste of time. In my estimation, the two most revealing objective data that could be obtained are body temperature and pulse rate.

The body temperature, for all intents, reflects the intensity of the metabolic rate, which, in turn, governs the amount of heat that is generated. Anything but merely a sign of excess food intake, the production of heat is needed to maintain the temperatures for the continued optimal functioning of all the enzymes in the body, and thus, processes such as tissue renewal and repair. After all, nearly all the food we eat is ultimately converted to heat, in one way or another. An intense metabolic rate also ensures a continuous supply of energy (while limiting the storage of the food we eat as fat), which is essential for the organization and functioning of all living cells.

The idea of maintaining a higher body temperature is controversial given Raymond Pearl's "rate of living" theory (discussed in chapter 3), which, if you recall, reflects a mechanical and unrealistic conception of organisms. In point of fact, conditions as diverse as obesity, diabetes, and senescence are associated with lower-than-normal diet-induced thermogenesis.[1]

The intolerance to cold is often disregarded, yet seems to be highly common among people, especially among women. From my own research and observations, cold intolerance – in the hands, feet, genitals, and nose – is among the most intolerable symptoms I've ever encountered. Keeping track of your body temperature (I recommend the axillary [armpit] temperature) every morning, afternoon (after lunch), and evening (before bed) for about a month will help to reveal your temperature rhythms, and therefore your state of health and metabolism. The famous "thyroidologist" Dr. Broda Barnes found that those temperature readings should hover around 97.8 to 98.6 degrees,[2] rising to a peak in the afternoon.

It is important to bear in mind that although the body temperature is a relatively accurate means of assessing your metabolism and state of health, it can be misleading because the stress hormones can also elevate the body temperature to apparently optimal levels – especially during times of intense stress. However, you can easily determine whether the stress hormones are keeping your body temperature up: If after eating breakfast your body temperature rapidly declines, then the stress hormones are at play, and you have some work to do.

The pulse rate, another self-diagnostic tool that complements the body temperature, reflects the rate at which the heart is pumping blood, oxygen, and nutrients to cells throughout the body. While many physicians subscribe to idea that "lower is better," they tend to justify this theory using athletes as shining examples. Besides the fact that it is not uncommon for athletes to spontaneously drop dead, a lower pulse rate is suggestive of reduced blood flow, which, in effect, limits the rate at which cells can generate energy. Similar to the body temperature, there are some caveats to a higher pulse rate. In stress, the pulse rate can be maintained by adrenaline, sometimes elevating the pulse rate to over 100 beats per minute (BPM). Instead of feeling pleasant, elevated adrenaline causes anxiety and poor sleep. In all, a pulse rate of about 85 BPM and body temperature of about 98.6 degrees are suggestive of high rates of efficient energy production, rather than a metabolism maintained by the stress hormones.

Suggestion #1: Adequate Protein

In 1985, the World Health Organization proposed a standard dietary protein requirement of 0.625 grams per kilogram of body weight per day and a "safe" level of 0.75 g/kg BW/d. In 1993, this recommendation was revised by researchers at MIT to 0.8 g/kg BW/d, which is the current recommendation. However, Army researchers concerned with the unique demands placed on soldiers in combat, including muscle mass and strength, response to injury, infection, environmental stress, and cognitive performance found the World Health Organization's standard recommendation of 0.8 g/kg BW/d to be inadequate for preventing nitrogen loss and undesirable changes in testosterone, IGF-1 and active thyroid hormone, triiodothyronine (T3). Improving upon the standard recommendation considerably, researchers found that 1.5 g/kg BW/d ameliorated various problems "stressed" soldiers were having with the standard recommendation.[3]

The general slowing of the metabolism seen in soldiers on low protein diets is analogous to many of the changes found in those with pattern baldness. A deficient protein intake commonly leads to hair loss, slowed growth and depigmentation (graying). Unsurprisingly, pattern baldness also seems to be associated with inadequate protein consumption to some degree.[4] However, the types of protein you choose is as important as the amount, in that if the protein's amino acid profile is unbalanced, or if the protein comes with excessive amounts of iron and polyunsaturated fats, it can actually contribute to pattern baldness.

Iron is found in a variety of proteins, including beef, bison, lamb and goat. Similar to polyunsaturated fats,[5,6] excess iron tends to accumulate in the tissues of both men and women throughout a lifetime. Iron continually damages cells by interfering with respiration and by oxidative stress. Like the polyunsaturated fats,[7] iron increases the need for antioxidants and depletes the vitamin E.[8] Rather than avoiding ruminant muscle meats altogether, because they provide high-quality protein, are low in PUFA and are easy to obtain, foods such as coffee and milk (for the calcium) can be used to inhibit iron absorption during or shortly after a meal containing these foods.

Another problem with fulfilling your protein requirements from muscle meats is their poor ratio of calcium to phosphate. The adaptive "stress" hormone, parathyroid hormone (PTH) is especially sensitive to this balance of minerals. Constance R. Martin, author of Endocrine Physiology (1985) stated, "...it is important to point out that low levels of PTH are essential for maintaining healthy bone structure and normal remodeling."[9] Naturally, calcium-rich proteins such as milk and cheese are ideal for balancing the ratio of calcium to phosphate, however, for some, these foods tend to be very allergenic.

While often considered a 'genetic-inherited-condition', there are several explanations for dairy allergy. For example, additives in milk and cheese (e.g., vitamins, enzymes, vegetable rennet) can be allergenic in themselves. Experimenting with milk deficient in added vitamins and cheeses with no additives (e.g., only salt, animal rennet and milk) might make a considerable difference in the allergenicity of these foods. Low thyroid, by causing an overgrowth of bacteria in the small intestines,[10] can contribute to the loss of the lactase enzyme.[11] If dairy remains to be intolerable, homemade calcium from eggshells is a safe supplement for increasing the ratio of calcium to phosphate and lowering PTH and prolactin.[12,13]

In addition to their iron content and poor calcium to phosphate ratio, the amino acid profile of ruminant muscle meats is of somewhat of a concern. An excess of the essential amino acids methionine, cysteine and tryptophan tend to have a few anti-metabolic inflammatory effects. For instance, tryptophan is the precursor to serotonin, which promotes many stress substances involved in the pathogenesis of balding (e.g., estrogen, cortisol, prolactin). Tryptophan is associated with aging hair, and accumulates more so than other amino acid in graying hair.[14] In contrast, protein sources that provide gelatin (e.g., oxtail, shanks, broth) are deficient in these problematic amino acids, and contain unusually large amounts of glycine and proline, which reduce several of the inflammatory markers associated with pattern baldness.[15,16]

To round out the protein from milk, cheese, and gelatinous cuts of meat, the diet should include various low-fat shellfish (especially oysters), liver (ruminant), and eggs. These foods provide significant amounts of the hard-to-get micronutrients such as zinc, selenium, vitamin A and copper, all of which are important for hair growth and likely deficient, to varying extents, in those with pattern baldness. (It is important to note that the requirement for all nutrients increase in proportion to the metabolic rate, as indicated by the pulse rate and body temperature).

Suggestion #2: Adequate Carbohydrate

In early 2000, researchers raised the question of whether insulin resistance was a mechanism or promoting factor in early pattern baldness.[17] Baldness is associated with a few hormones that interfere with glucose metabolism and insulin signaling. Estrogen is associated with balding[18] and interferes with glucose metabolism.[19] Another hormone, prolactin, which is increased by estrogen, has been referred to as a "diabetogenic hormone."[20] Both estrogen and prolactin increase the pituitary's release of adrenocorticotrophic hormone (ACTH), which invariably leads to cortisol production. Cortisol independently induces insulin resistance[21] and was found to be "significantly higher" in both men and women with pattern hair loss.[22] Estrogen, prolactin, and cortisol are known to cause loss of sodium from the extracellular fluid increasing the "salt retaining" hormone, aldosterone. Aldosterone was found to be elevated in both men and women with premature hair loss[23] and induces insulin resistance in healthy people.[24]

Using a bioenergetic model of pattern baldness we find that a "higher functioning" of various adaptive "stress" substances is preceded by "inefficient" cellular energy metabolism. While the mainstream medical culture claims "sugar causes diabetes," sucrose, and more specifically, fructose (sucrose is half fructose half glucose) is the most effective carbohydrate for supporting oxidative mitochondrial metabolism. For instance, fructose, more so than glucose, increases the production of carbon dioxide.[25] Fructose also helps when carbohydrate metabolism has been interfered with by bypassing a step in glucose metabolism that is inhibited by free fatty acids for continued oxidative metabolism. Researchers recently found that fructose was "cytoprotective" against cyanide, which is toxic to cells.[26] Similarly, in another experiment, fructose was able to protect liver cells in a low oxygen environment by opposing various shifts that appear during stress.[27]

The universally negative view of fructose appears to be an outgrowth of the draconian view of cholesterol put forth by Ancel Keys and John Yudkin in the early 1970s. In John Yudkin's book, *Pure, White & Deadly*, he stated, "Fructose seems to be the part of sucrose that produces most of the ill-effects of sucrose" and believed that the overconsumption of sucrose produced unfavorable changes in blood lipids that led to heart disease (i.e., the lipid hypothesis). Uffe Ravnskov, Dr. Chris Masterjohn, and others have refuted the lipid hypothesis in finding that there's no connection between saturated fat, cholesterol, and heart disease. However, elevated cholesterol is closely related with low thyroid[28] and along with vitamin A the three substances are used to synthesize the "youth-associated" steroid-precursor, pregnenolone. In an adaptive process, cholesterol increases during stress to provide the raw material for steroid synthesis. For example, in an experiment with college students, cholesterol levels went up before exams, and returned to normal shortly after the exam.[29] If cholesterol levels were too low, common among violent criminals and those with depression and suicidal tendencies, the most efficient way to normalize cholesterol levels would be to consume more fructose, "the most lipogenic carbohydrate."

The most common criticism launched at fructose is that fructose is shunted directly to the liver where it is converted to fat, setting the stage for fatty liver disease (NAFLD), diabetes and obesity. While it is true that the liver rapidly uses fructose, it does so primarily to refill the liver's sugar supply in the form of glycogen. In one study, an infusion of fructose resulted in about 360 percent more hepatic glycogen than a glucose infusion.[30] The liver's glycogen storage capacity is very large. One study suggested that "de novo lipogenesis [DNL] is not an important pathway in humans" and that chronic overfeeding on carbohydrates increased glycogen stores of about 500 grams before DNL became significant.[31] To clarify, only with chronic overfeeding and saturated glycogen stores does the conversion of carbohydrate to fat become significant. While usually mentioned in the context of athleticism, hepatic glycogen is an important health factor for everyone. Adequately "stocking" the liver's reserve of glycogen is central in resisting maladaptation to long-term adaptive "stress" hormones like adrenaline, glucagon, and cortisol. For instance, cortisol levels in wild monkeys who consume a diet of primarily fruit, increase when their diets contain less sugar.[32] Similarly, sugar lowers the main pituitary hormone, ACTH, which signals the production of cortisol.[33]

In contrast to the beneficial effects of fruits, starchy carbohydrates (e.g., grains, breads, pastas and legumes) are a problematic carbohydrate source. On average, glucose and fructose are found together in the form of sucrose, which seem to compliment each other. However, glucose alone, as found predominantly in starch, appears to be inflammatory. In a study comparing the effects of glucose and fructose, fructose more so than glucose increased dietary thermogenesis, which is impaired in obesity, diabetes and old age.[34] In another study, it was demonstrated that when compared to fructose and alcohol, glucose increased the generation of reactive oxygen species (ROS) and the inflammatory marker NF-κB in healthy volunteers.[35] Increased generation of ROS is associated with baldness[36] and NF-κB inhibits the production of testosterone[37] and progesterone.[38] Equally, a couple of years later the same group showed that glucose ingestion in humans raised levels of TNF-α — another inflammatory marker associated with baldness.[39,40] Starches tend to increase inflammatory parathyroid hormone (PTH), while fruit suppresses it. In addition to having a favorable calcium to phosphate ratio, fructose lowers serum phosphate[41] and decreases its absorption from the intestine.[42] Fructose also seems to enhance the retention of the minerals involved in restraining the synthesis of PTH, including magnesium and copper.[43]

Some have progressed the idea of "safe starches" suggesting that potatoes, sweet potatoes, taro, and other tubers are "optimal" sources of carbohydrate. Indeed, when cooked generously and peeled, potatoes are a nutrient-dense food containing high quality protein. However, they still provide enough starch to cause problems in sensitive individuals. Starch—regardless of the source—tends to cause problems with bacterial endotoxin.[44] On the other hand, the sugar in fruit is rapidly digested and absorbed equally as rapidly in the upper small intestines, where endotoxin is not a concern.

Due to their unfavorable calcium to phosphate ratio, relatively high iron content, and negative effects on bacterial endotoxin, starches, from grains, breads, pastas and legumes, should be avoided. In contrast, sugar, found in fruits, fruit juices, honey and dairy, is relatively deficient in iron and unsaturated fats; they also have a favorable calcium to phosphate ratio and the protective and supportive fructose. In my estimation, fruit is the ideal carbohydrate source.

Suggestion #3: Become Deficient in The "Essential Fatty Acids"

When a healthy cell is stimulated, the mitochondria become more active, and may require more energy than is immediately available from free glucose, glycogen, or the creatinine-phosphocreatine system.

As a "backup fuel," free fatty acids are liberated from adipose tissue into the blood by the stress hormones. These free fatty acids can be formed into triglycerides, converted into ketone bodies, or remain as free fatty acids in the blood. While the formation of ketone bodies has some protective effects, they are produced in a state of metabolic stress. Wolfe, et al. noted that "the enhanced mobilization and oxidation of fat is one of the fundamental responses to stress" and that there was "little doubt that there are signals for the increased mobilization of fat [present] in shock, trauma, and sepsis."[45] An increased concentration of free fatty acids in the blood, especially the unsaturated variety, interferes with the metabolism of glucose and the mitochondrial consumption of oxygen in the short- and long-term.

The immediate function of free fatty acids is to interfere with the uptake and oxidation of glucose. This observation was first made by British biochemist Sir Phillip Randle in the early 1960s and is sometimes called the "Randle cycle".[46] In the long-term, free fatty acids have been referred to as a "toxic candidate" for the insulin-secreting pancreatic beta cells.[47] In fact, it was found that chronic exposure to even moderate amounts of fatty acids dysregulates and impairs the functioning of the beta cells, even destroying them in severe cases.[48] Another long-term negative effect of elevated free fatty acids is their tendency to interfere with the production, transport, and activation of thyroid hormones,[49] which regulate oxidative metabolism. Unsaturated fats cause pathological changes in the mitochondria, too. Raymond Peat, PhD has brought attention to cardiolipin, a saturated (double) phospholipid found exclusively in the mitochondria. In physical proximity, cardiolipin supports the activity of the cytochrome c oxidase, an enzyme that occupies the last crucial step in the process of "efficient" oxidative energy metabolism. It was found that this enzyme's activity changes, "specifically [by] an increase in highly unsaturated fatty acids."[50]

The largest contribution of dietary fats to the genesis of pattern baldness is probably their degradation into hormone-like inflammatory substances called prostaglandins. While prostaglandins are often said to be both "good" and "bad," in a bioenergetic view of baldness they seem to be exclusively bad. Prostaglandins interfere directly with oxidative mitochondrial metabolism,[51] reducing concentrations of carbon dioxide and increasing lactic acid. The prostaglandins tend to increase concentrations of estrogen and prolactin,[52,53] which are both associated with pattern hair loss.[54,55] Recently, it was found that balding men had increased levels of prostaglandin D2 in their scalps;[56] reinforcing the general view of baldness as an inflammatory disorder. Fish oil is often considered "anti-inflammatory" owing to the interference of prostaglandin synthesis by eicosapentaenoic acid (EPA). However, these fats are so unstable that they spontaneously decompose (if they haven't decomposed already) in the body, and their breakdown products, in themselves, are highly and directly toxic, especially with regard to the interest of pattern baldness.

By comparison, saturated fats are a safer source of calories by simply containing less of the unsaturated fats, but they also have various pro-metabolic effects, too. For instance, medium-chain triglycerides (concentrated in coconut fats) are more easily oxidized for energy than long chain fatty acids providing energy when glucose metabolism has been interfered with. Similarly, saturated fats support the pyruvate dehydrogenase enzyme (PDH) that links glycolysis to the Krebs cycle.[57] In contrast, PDH is inhibited by the polyunsaturated fats.[58] Saturated fats appear to protect against the detrimental effects of bacterial endotoxin, fortifying the intestinal barrier.[59] Fats such as coconut oil, butter, and ruminant animal fat and cocoa are all highly saturated and safe sources of calories. It should be noted that most all restaurants cook with cheap PUFA-laced oils. When eating out, a small amount of vitamin E (topically or orally) may provide a minimal amount of protection from these fats.

Supplements

Salt - Stressed, deenergized cells accumulate intracellular sodium and rapidly lose extracellular sodium. This hypotonic (i.e., sodium deficient) state in the blood increases the secretion of aldosterone by the adrenal glands and the fat cells. While life-saving in the short-term, aldosterone is inflammatory in excess and has been found to be elevated in those with pattern baldness.[60] Consuming less salt than what your appetite calls for provokes the release of aldosterone, too, and releases the brake on the secretion of adrenaline and noradrenaline, raising the levels of these two stress hormones in parallel with aldosterone.

Aldosterone, adrenaline, and noradrenaline worsen insulin sensitivity[61] (even in healthy subjects) and increase various factors associated with baldness. Adequate dietary salt, by suppressing aldosterone, adrenalin, and noradrenalin, helps to dampen the stress response. Aldosterone appears to increase when salt intake drops below 1.5 teaspoons per day.[62] Although boutique salts have become popular of late, the more inexpensive canning and pickling salts, which lack iron, are probably the safest of all the options.

Coffee - Coffee is often referred to as an addictive drug akin to a narcotic. This point of view is irrational and irrelevant as coffee parallels thyroid and progesterone in supporting "efficient" respiratory energy. For instance, coffee provides hard-to-get energy co-factors, including riboflavin, niacin and magnesium. Magnesium is of particular interest as it works together with T3 to generate and retain ATP in the cell. Caffeine itself is beneficial, protecting against cancer[63] and liver injury,[64] and reducing prolactin.[65] In addition, coffee can be used to inhibit iron absorption during a meal or up to an hour after the meal.[66] Because coffee stimulates the metabolism, it should be consumed with meals to avoid low blood sugar.

Vitamin D - A common nutrient deficiency,[67] Vitamin D is an important factor for regulating hair follicle cycling.[68] Vitamin D has antiestrogenic qualities,[69] and prolactin, which is increased by estrogen, decreases rapidly during vitamin D therapy.[70] Vitamins A, E and K work synergistically with D and are also antiestrogenic.[71,72,73] When sufficient amounts of vitamin D are present, renin, and therefore the stress hormone aldosterone, is suppressed.[74] The main source of vitamin D is sun exposure. Depending on location this can be difficult, which is why vitamin D supplementation may be necessary. In a recent study it was found that serum levels of at least 40 ng/dL were needed to limit PTH secretion.[75] The correct blood test for assessing vitamin D status is 25-hydroxycholecalciferol, or 25-hydroxyvitamin D.

Review

In no particular order here is a review of the recommendations mentioned above. Cronometer.com is a useful tool for figuring out some of the more nuanced suggestions (i.e., calcium to phosphate ratio).

Adequate Protein – A modifier of 1.5 grams of protein per kilogram of body weight can be used to experiment with protein intake. Depending on activity and stress level, some may need more. Given that protein is insulinogenic, consuming more protein during the day and less at night seems reasonable. Sources of protein include, milk, cheese and gelatinous cuts of meat. Supplemental proteins include ruminant liver, shellfish (especially oysters), and eggs (specifically the yolks).

Adequate Carbohydrate – Due to the

insulinogenic nature of protein, carbohydrate intake should exceed protein intake. Meat and carbohydrate can be balanced in a 1:1 ratio, while dairy warrants a ratio of 2-3:1 due to its greater stimulation of insulin. Ripe fruits such as oranges, tangerines, watermelon, grapes, lemons, limes, cherries, sapotas, guavas, lychees, papayas, and other citrus and tropical fruits provide enough glucose and fructose for general stress resistance. In addition, these fruits tend to contain low levels of serotonin, which can be problematic in sensitive individuals. Fruit supports respiration, contains low levels of iron and polyunsaturated fats, and contains a favorable calcium to phosphate ratio. Starches such as grains, breads, and beans contain enough iron and phosphate to greatly limit their consumption or eliminate them all together. Additionally, fruit is digested in the upper part of the intestine avoiding complications with bacterial endotoxin, while starches tend to promote the absorption of endotoxin into the blood.

Become Deficient in The EFAs – A diet based on nutrient-dense proteins and fruits tends to automatically limit the amount of polyunsaturated fats in the diet. Coconut oil, butter, animal fats and cocoa are all highly saturated and safe to consume. Olive oil contains enough unsaturated fat to warrant limiting its consumption. Vegetable and seed oils should be avoided completely. Similarly, the highly unsaturated fats found in fish and flax oils (i.e., the so-called "essential fatty acids") are not recommended.

Supplements – A majority of dietary supplements are not recommended due to their allergenicity and poor manufacturing quality. Food supplements such as salt (to taste), ruminant liver (once or twice a week), oysters (a few times a week or everyday), and eggs (everyday) are highly recommended. Vitamin D is an important regulator of hair health and exposing as much of the body to sunlight without burning as possible is desirable. Cycles of light and darkness seem to have a dramatic effect on hair growth. For example, 90% of hair follicles shift from the resting to growing phase during springtime only to fall out in winter months.[76] This phenomenon may be explained by light exposure, which as many have suspected, is biologically active. Low-level laser therapy makes use of red light initiating regrowth of hair in some individuals.[77] A physiological mechanism for light's effect on hair growth may have to do with its inhibition of the "molting" hormone, prolactin, which is sensitive to light and increased in darkness.[78] For those that cannot spend a significant amount of time in the sun supplementing with vitamin D (if less than ~40 ng/dL) and utilizing red light (600-850nm) around one's workspace may be warranted.

References

1. Tappy, L, and Jéquier, E. Fructose and dietary thermogenesis. Am J Clin Nutr. 1993 Nov;58(5 Suppl):766S-770S.
2. Barnes, O. Hypothyroidism: The Unsuspecting Illness. 1976
3. Committee of Military Nutritional Research. The Role of Protein and Amino Acids in Sustaining and Enhancing Performance. 1999
4. El Fékih, N., et al. [Evaluation of the role of dietary intake in the occurrence of alopecia]. Rev Med Liege. 2010 Feb;65(2):98-102.
5. Nourooz-Zadeh, J., and Pereira, P. Age-related accumulation of free polyunsaturated fatty acids in human retina. Ophthalmic Res. 1999;31(4):273-9.
6. Laganiere, S. and Yu, B.P. Modulation of membrane phospholipid fatty acid composition by age and food restriction. Gerontology. 1993;39(1):7-18.
7. Valk, E.E., and Hornstra, G. Relationship between vitamin E requirement and polyunsaturated fatty acid intake in man: a review. Int J Vitam Nutr Res. 2000 Mar;70(2):31-42.
8. Galleano, M. and Puntarulo, S. Mild iron overload effect on rat liver nuclei. Toxicology. 1994 Nov 11;93(2-3):125-34.
9. Martin, C. Endocrine Physiology. 1985. "...it is important to point out that low levels of PTH are essential for maintaining healthy bone structure and normal remodeling."
10. Lauritano, E.C., et al. Association between hypothyroidism and

small intestinal bacterial overgrowth. J Clin Endocrinol Metab. 2007 Nov;92(11):4180-4. Epub 2007 Aug 14.

11. Walshe, K., et al. Effects of an enteric anaerobic bacterial culture supernatant and deoxycholate on intestinal calcium absorption and disaccharidase activity. Gut. 1990 Jul;31(7):770-6.

12. Schaafsma, A., et al. Mineral, amino acid, and hormonal composition of chicken eggshell powder and the evaluation of its use in human nutrition. Poult Sci. 2000 Dec;79(12):1833-8.

13. Rovenský, J., et al. Eggshell calcium in the prevention and treatment of osteoporosis. Int J Clin Pharmacol Res. 2003;23(2-3):83-92.

14. Bertazzo, A., et al. Tryptophan in human hair: correlation with pigmentation. Farmaco. 2000 Aug;55(8):521-5.

15. Wheeler, M.D., and Thurman, R.G. Production of superoxide and TNF-alpha from alveolar macrophages is blunted by glycine. Am J Physiol. 1999 Nov;277(5 Pt 1):L952-9.

16. Wheeler, M.D., et al. Dietary glycine blunts lung inflammatory cell influx following acute endotoxin. Am J Physiol Lung Cell Mol Physiol. 2000 Aug;279(2):L390-8.

17. Matilainen, V., et al. Early androgenetic alopecia as a marker of insulin resistance. Lancet. 2000 Sep 30;356(9236):1165-6.

18. Schmidt, J.B., et al. Hormonal parameters in androgenetic hair loss in the male. Dermatologica. 1991;182(4):214-7.

19. Goodman, M.N., and Hazelwood, R.L. Short-term effects of oestradiol benzoate in normal, hypophysectomized and alloxan-diabetic male rats. J Endocrinol. 1974 Sep;62(3):439-49.

20. Landgraf, R., et al. Prolactin: a diabetogenic hormone. Diabetologia. 1977 Apr;13(2):99-104.

21. Lager, I. The insulin-antagonistic effect of the counterregulatory hormones. J Intern Med Suppl. 1991;735:41-7.

22. Schmidt, J.B. Hormonal basis of male and female androgenic alopecia: clinical relevance. Skin Pharmacol. 1994;7(1-2):61-6.

23. Arias-Santiago, S., et al. Androgenetic alopecia and cardiovascular risk factors in men and women: a comparative study. J Am Acad Dermatol. 2010 Sep;63(3):420-9.

24. Garg, R., Low-salt diet increases insulin resistance in healthy subjects. Metabolism. 2011 Jul;60(7):965-8.

25. Brundin, T., and Wahren, J. Whole body and splanchnic oxygen consumption and blood flow after oral ingestion of fructose or glucose. Am J Physiol. 1993 Apr;264(4 Pt 1):E504-13.

26. Niknahad, H., et al. Prevention of cyanide-induced cytotoxicity by nutrients in isolated rat hepatocytes. Toxicol Appl Pharmacol. 1994 Oct;128(2):271-9.

27. Niknahad, H., et al. Hepatocyte injury resulting from the inhibition of mitochondrial respiration at low oxygen concentrations involves reductive stress and oxygen activation. Chem Biol Interact. 1995 Oct 20;98(1):27-44.

28. Sundaram, V., et al. Both hypothyroidism and hyperthyroidism enhance low density lipoprotein oxidation. J Clin Endocrinol Metab. 1997 Oct;82(10):3421-4.

29. Grundry, S.M., and Griffin, A.C. Effects of periodic mental stress on serum cholesterol levels. Circulation. 1959 Apr;19(4):496-8

30. Nilsson, L.H., and Hultman E. Liver and muscle glycogen in man after glucose and fructose infusion. Scand J Clin Lab Invest. 1974 Feb;33(1):5-10.

31. Acheson, K.J., et al. Glycogen storage capacity and de novo lipogenesis during massive carbohydrate overfeeding in man. Am J Clin Nutr. 1988 Aug;48(2):240-7.

32. Behie, A.M., et al. Sources of variation in fecal cortisol levels in howler monkeys in Belize. Am J Primatol. 2010 Jun;72(7):600-6.

33. Ulrich-Lai, Y.M., et al. HPA axis dampening by limited sucrose intake: reward frequency vs. caloric consumption. Physiol Behav. 2011 Apr 18;103(1):104-10.

34. Tappy, L, and Jéquier, E. Fructose and dietary thermogenesis. Am J Clin Nutr. 1993 Nov;58(5 Suppl):766S-770S.

35. Dhindsa, S., et al. Differential effects of glucose and alcohol on reactive oxygen species generation and intranuclear nuclear factor-kappaB in mononuclear cells. Metabolism. 2004 Mar;53(3):330-4.

36. Giralt, M., et al. Glutathione, glutathione S-transferase and reactive oxygen species of human scalp sebaceous glands in male pattern baldness. J Invest Dermatol. 1996 Aug;107(2):154-8.

37. Hong, C.Y., et al. Molecular mechanism of suppression of testicular steroidogenesis by proinflammatory cytokine tumor necrosis factor alpha.

38. Allport, V.C., et al. Human labour is associated with nuclear factor-kappaB activity which mediates cyclo-oxygenase-2 expression and is involved with the 'functional progesterone withdrawal'. Mol Hum Reprod. 2001 Jun;7(6):581-6.

39. Aljada, A., et al. Glucose ingestion induces an increase in intranuclear nuclear factor kappaB, a fall in cellular inhibitor kappaB, and an increase in tumor necrosis factor alpha messenger RNA by mononuclear cells in healthy human subjects. Metabolism. 2006 Sep;55(9):1177-85.

40. Philpott, M.P., et al. Effects of interleukins, colony-stimulating factor and tumour necrosis factor on human hair follicle growth in vitro: a possible role for interleukin-1 and tumour necrosis factor-alpha in alopecia areata. Br J Dermatol. 1996 Dec;135(6):942-8.

41. Kapur S. A medical hypothesis: phosphorus balance and prostate cancer. Cancer Invest. 2000;18(7):664-9.

42. Kirchner, S., et al. Luminal fructose inhibits rat intestinal sodium-phosphate cotransporter gene expression and phosphate uptake.

Am J Clin Nutr. 2008 Apr;87(4):1028-38.

43. Holbrook, J.T., et al. Dietary fructose or starch: effects on copper, zinc, iron, manganese, calcium, and magnesium balances in humans. Am J Clin Nutr. 1989 Jun;49(6):1290-4.

44. Ghanim, H., et al. Orange juice neutralizes the proinflammatory effect of a high-fat, high-carbohydrate meal and prevents endotoxin increase and Toll-like receptor expression. Am J Clin Nutr. 2010 Apr;91(4):940-9.

45. Wolfe, R.R., et al. Energy metabolism in trauma and sepsis: the role of fat. Prog Clin Biol Res. 1983;111:89-109.

46. Hue, L., and Taegtmeyer, H. The Randle cycle revisited: a new head for an old hat. Am J Physiol Endocrinol Metab. 2009 Sep;297(3):E578-91.

47. Li N, Frigerio F, Maechler P. The sensitivity of pancreatic beta-cells to mitochondrial injuries triggered by lipotoxicity and oxidative stress. Biochem Soc Trans. 2008 Oct;36(Pt 5):930-4.

48. Piro, S., et al. Chronic exposure to free fatty acids or high glucose induces apoptosis in rat pancreatic islets: possible role of oxidative stress. Metabolism. 2002 Oct;51(10):1340-7.

49. Clarke, S.D., and Hembree, J. Inhibition of triiodothyronine's induction of rat liver lipogenic enzymes by dietary fat. J Nutr. 1990 Jun;120(6):625-30.

50. Lee, H.J., et al. Selective remodeling of cardiolipin fatty acids in the aged rat heart. Lipids Health Dis. 2006 Jan 23;5:2.

51. Cherkasskaia, M.D., et al. [Effect of prostaglandin E2 on energy metabolism in isolated rat liver mitochondria]. Vopr Med Khim. 1982 May-Jun;28(3):110-4.

52. Bulun, S.E., et al. Estrogen biosynthesis in endometriosis: molecular basis and clinical relevance. J Mol Endocrinol. 2000 Aug;25(1):35-42.

53. Goldberg, V.J., and Ramwell, P.W. Role of prostaglandins in reproduction. Physiol Rev. 1975 Jul;55(3):325-51.

54. Schmidt, J.B., et al. Hormonal parameters in androgenetic hair loss in the male. Dermatologica. 1991;182(4):214-7.

55. Schmidt, J.B., et al.[Hyperprolactinemia and hypophyseal hypothyroidism as cofactors in hirsutism and androgen-induced alopecia in women]. Hautarzt. 1991 Mar;42(3):168-72.

56. Garza, L.A., et al. Prostaglandin d2 inhibits hair growth and is elevated in bald scalp of men with androgenetic alopecia. Sci Transl Med. 2012 Mar 21;4(126):126ra34.

57. Humphries, K.M., and Szweda, L.I. Selective inactivation of alpha-ketoglutarate dehydrogenase and pyruvate dehydrogenase: reaction of lipoic acid with 4-hydroxy-2-nonenal. Biochemistry. 1998 Nov 10;37(45):15835-41.

58. Bradley, N.S., et al. The acute effects of differential dietary fatty acids on human skeletal muscle pyruvate dehydrogenase activity.

59. Nanji, A.A., et al. Dietary saturated fatty acids down-regulate cyclooxygenase-2 and tumor necrosis factor alfa and reverse fibrosis in alcohol-induced liver disease in the rat. Hepatology. 1997 Dec;26(6):1538-45.

60. Arias-Santiago, S., et al. Androgenetic alopecia and cardiovascular risk factors in men and women: a comparative study. J Am Acad Dermatol. 2010 Sep;63(3):420-9.

61. Garg, R., Low-salt diet increases insulin resistance in healthy subjects. Metabolism. 2011 Jul;60(7):965-8.

62. Alderman, M.H., et al. Association of the renin-sodium profile with the risk of myocardial infarction in patients with hypertension. N Engl J Med. 1991 Apr 18;324(16):1098-104.

63. Würzner, H.P., et al. A 2-year feeding study of instant coffees in rats. II. Incidence and types of neoplasms. Food Cosmet Toxicol. 1977 Aug;15(4):289-96.

64. Sakamoto, W., et al. Coffee and fitness-coffee suppresses lipopolysaccharide-induced liver injury in rats. J Nutr Sci Vitaminol (Tokyo). 2000 Dec;46(6):316-20.

65. Casas, M., et al. Dopaminergic mechanism for caffeine-induced decrease in fertility? Lancet. 1989 Apr 1;1(8640):731.

66. Morck, T.A., et al. Inhibition of food iron absorption by coffee. Am J Clin Nutr March 1983 vol. 37 no. 3 416-420

67. Holick, M.F. Vitamin D deficiency. N Engl J Med. 2007 Jul 19;357(3):266-81.

68. Bikle, D.D., et al. Development and progression of alopecia in the vitamin D receptor null mouse. J Cell Physiol. 2006 May;207(2):340-53.

69. Krishnan, A.V., et al. Vitamin D and breast cancer: inhibition of estrogen synthesis and signaling. J Steroid Biochem Mol Biol. 2010 Jul;121(1-2):343-8. Epub 2010 Feb 13.

70. Verbeelen, D., et al. Effect of 1,25-dihydroxyvitamin D3 on plasma prolactin in patients with renal failure on regular dialysis treatment. J Endocrinol Invest. 1983 Oct;6(5):359-62.

71. BO, W.J. Relation of vitamin A deficiency and estrogen to induction of keratinizing metaplasia in the uterus of the rat. Am J Clin Nutr. 1957 Nov-Dec;5(6):666-73.

72. Otsuka, M., et al. Vitamin K2 binds 17beta-hydroxysteroid dehydrogenase 4 and modulates estrogen metabolism. Life Sci. 2005 Apr 8;76(21):2473-82.

73. Briggs, M. Letter: Vitamin E status and oral contraceptives. Am J Clin Nutr. 1975 May;28(5):436.

74. Forman, J.P., et al. Plasma 25-hydroxyvitamin D and regulation of the renin-angiotensin system in humans. Hypertension. 2010 May;55(5):1283-8. Epub 2010 Mar 29.

75. Ginde, A.A., et al. Defining vitamin D status by secondary hyperparathyroidism in the U.S. population. J Endocrinol

Invest. 2012 Jan;35(1):42-8. Epub 2011 May 23.

76. Randall, VA, and Ebling, F.J. Seasonal changes in human hair growth. Br J Dermatol. 1991 Feb;124(2):146-51.

77. Bouzari, N, and Firooz, A.R. Lasers may induce terminal hair growth. Dermatol Surg. 2006 Mar;32(3):460.

78. Freeman, M.E., et al. Prolactin: structure, function, and regulation of secretion. Physiol Rev. 2000 Oct;80(4):1523-631.

THE FUTURE

"Aged? But he does not appear aged, just look, his hair has
remained young!"
—Marcel Proust (In Search of Lost Time, 1913-27)

During the five years I worked as a technician for a youth-centered computer company, I noticed that my peers were balding at an alarming rate. In fact, early baldness was so common among the 20-something employee base (and the clientele) that customers would bring it up regularly while I worked on their computers.

In addition to spending my shifts observing people's hairlines, my identity as "the hair guy" allowed me to engage in unprovoked conversations with coworkers concerned with their hair. Often, the loss of hair coincided with revelations of depression, anxiety, constipation and low libido. Because I had experienced similar problems, these interactions cemented pattern baldness as a systemic issue rather than a compartmentalized problem.

The most revealing of these interactions happened during a year I worked closely with a fellow who was becoming a woman. Aesthetically, he had nice features, but his hair was on another level. His thick, long blonde hair could only be described as radiant. However, this changed, quickly, when he adopted hormone replacement therapy (HRT). Large doses of estrogen along with smaller amounts of synthetic progesterone caused his luxurious hair to dim. During the course of six months, his hair became course, dull and began to noticeably thin. His disposition, however, was unaffected, as his transformation into a woman brought him great jubilation.

Events such as these helped shape my current understanding of pattern hair loss. Discussions about whether a person's hair loss is androgenic, androgen-independent, or age-related have neglected the possibility that pattern hair loss does not begin in advanced age or when a genetic code is triggered. Rather, pattern hair loss—of any kind—is the result of a life-long development process involving stress, energy and aging.

ABOUT THE AUTHOR & COACHING

Danny Roddy is an independent health researcher based in San Francisco, California. You can find all of his work on dannyroddy.com

If you need help incorporating the ideas in this book, please visit: dannyroddy.com/coaching

16940897R00064

Made in the USA
Middletown, DE
29 December 2014